Barry S. Giddens

●━━━━━━━━━━━━━━━━━━━━━━●

Rebuild Bible Study:
Core Christian Values
for
Church
and
Personal Success

●━━━━━━━━━━━━━━━━━━━━━━●

www.RebuildBook.com

Maple Publishing
MaplePublishing.online

REBUILD BIBLE STUDY:
Core Christian Values for Church and Personal Success

Copyright © 2017 by Barry S. Giddens

ISBN: 978-0-9987903-6-7
E-book ISBN: 978-0-9987903-7-4

God placed a great desire in my heart to see souls won for Christ at an early age. I dedicate this book to my grandfather, Francis E. Allen, Rev. Charles E. Culbreth, Rev. Tegler Greer, and Dr. Max Hill. They were all simple men, but their faith in God has inspired me to be a man of faith, ever growing my relationship with our Lord.

Contents

Taking Sides and Drawing Lines in the Sand:
CHURCH IS ABOUT JESUS

SECTION TWO: FOCUS ON THE INDIVIDUAL

Introduction
Rebuild Bible Study:
Core Christian Values for
Church and Personal Success

Quote:

"Give me one hundred men who fear nothing but sin and desire nothing but God, and I care not whether they be clergyman or laymen, they alone will shake the gates of Hell and set up the kingdom of Heaven upon the earth."

– John Wesley[1]

Scripture:

"And now, Israel, what does the Lord your God ask of you but to fear the Lord your God, to walk in obedience to him, to love him, to serve the Lord your God with all your heart and with all your soul"

- Deuteronomy 10:12 (NIV)

THE USS CONSTITUTION IS A MODERN MARVEL. Built 200 plus years ago by George Washington, it has the distinction of winning every war that it ever fought against the French, British, and pirates just after the formation of our new nation. From 1794 until 1815, each captain who took the helm

---

1   "Ministry and Religion." Ohio Christian University. http://www.ohiochristian.edu/ministry (May 21, 2014).

received a gold medal from the US Congress because of his success on the high seas. From 1815 until her decommissioning in 1855, the Constitution never fired a shot. She enjoyed a peaceful transition from war to her eventual status as a floating American museum. Today, "Old Ironsides" (as she was affectionately named) now graces locations around the world as a proud representation of America's past.

East Macon United Methodist Church in Macon, Georgia, was a beautiful white wooden building with black shutters situated close to the Ocmulgee River in downtown Macon, Georgia. The church dates back to the 1800's. While I remember passing by the church as a child, it closed several years ago. The building is now home to Word and Deed Ministries. In my first year at Lyons First United Methodist Church, I attended an estate sale in Vidalia, Georgia, some two hours from the location of East Macon UMC. As I walked through the house to see what might be of interest to me, I noticed a plate sitting on a dining room table among hundreds of other china plates. It said simply, "East Macon United Methodist Church." It had a black and white sketch of the church building.

While I do not know the circumstance of the lady who owned the plate, I can only imagine. After all, church plates were often created as a symbol of pride in one's hometown church. They were proudly displayed in the china cabinet as a badge of honor. Perhaps this lady grew up in East Macon UMC and she placed an order years ago for the plate. Even though the church was long gone, her pride remained for her church. When she first received the plate many years ago, she had no idea that one day the plate would be the only memory left from the church she once called "home."

We live in an ever-changing world. While our principles do not change, the way in which we do ministry must change with culture. Old Ironsides was a beast of a ship in the 1790's. While the British collectively were much better equipped, no British ship could individually match the Constitution. Even so, by 1855, the American Navy decommissioned her in order to keep up with an ever-changing world and a Civil War that would be decided largely because of the North's ability to adapt its Navy. The North succeeded in an effective naval blockade of the South, but Old Ironsides was nowhere to be found. If we could ask some of the Civil War sailors if they ever had the privilege of serving on the Constitution, I'm sure some would proudly say, "YES!" If we were to ask those same sailors if they would want to be found on the Constitution in the 1863 battle of Vicksburg, Mississippi against the South, they would collectively say, "NOT ON YOUR LIFE!"

For all that we do not know about East Macon UMC, we do know this: It did not keep up with the times. It surely had a heart for Jesus and a desire to win souls. In some of the committee meetings, the building was of great importance as was the desire to honor the existing members. They went through the same political infighting that we experience today in many of our churches. Surely people took sides over whether or not to buy a new organ or to paint the building. With the reality of church members' deaths and lack of church growth, East Macon UMC became nothing more than a black and white church sketch on a porcelain plate.

Section One will focus on holistic church growth. The challenge for existing churches in today's society is two-fold. First, it must win new converts for Jesus. Nothing grieves my soul more than when I see churches swap members who already know Jesus. While some do come to my church because they move into the community from another church, or they weren't active in another church, church swapping pulls from one church to make another church stronger . . . it's a "less for them is more for me" mentality. While the numbers look good on paper, there's one big problem . . . It doesn't make Jesus happy. When my son, Maddux, prays too loudly or doesn't complete the prayer, my mother will tell him, "Do it again . . . and this time make Jesus happy!" It's such an important lesson in life. We may cook the books in our churches and pack the pews, but unless it is found upon the reality that we need to make disciples of non-Christians, it misses the mark. Sin, simply defined is, "Missing the mark."

The second challenge that we must face is the reworking of existing structures to keep up with the times. Many of our current structures date back to the 1950's . . . the age of the mighty "organization." We no longer live in a world that values the organization. Denominationalism as a whole (Methodist, Baptist, Presbyterian, and Catholic) is on the decline.

The churches that are flourishing today are often independent of denominational structures or are very large (300+ member) denominational churches. Some bright spots exist in denominations where change is present. These churches embrace Jesus and cast off the need to be program-oriented or to do it that way because "That's the way we've always done it!" They understand that doing it the same old way is no longer going to work. They value authenticity among members and make sure that deep relationships are present. They nurture new opportunities for people to come to worship and realize that a church building is just that . . . a building. An old phrase says, "The church is not a building or a steeple; the church is THE PEOPLE!"

Topics in Section Two will focus on our growth as individual Christians. It is important for us to have a vibrant Bible study and prayer life. We must engage our physical health to make sure that we stay in the game. God wants us to take Sabbath rest at least one day each week. Valuing our relationship with Christ means also valuing our families. As a Christian, God wants us to share the message of Christ with others through personal evangelism. Section Two is a challenge to grow into the person that God has created us to become within a world that is ever-changing. As we grow as Christians, we become better equipped to lead our churches to the change that will bring about long-term vitality. Session Twelve is "Personal Evangelism." It will give you an opportunity for you to commit your life to Christ. No other commitment is more important during our time on earth. Our salvation directly affects our happiness and our eternal destination. Make a commitment to follow Christ today or to recommit your life to Christ. In all facets of your life, share Christ.

My prayer for this Bible study is that it will push us forward in our thinking. Each chapter in the book is relatively short. It contains seven church and five individual keys to success. *The Rebuild Bible Study* is a challenge for us to overcome our current circumstances as we experience life-changing church and personal growth. 1 John 4:4 (NIV) says, "You, dear children, are from God and have overcome them, because the one who is in you is greater than the one who is in the world." God does not want us just to exist or maintain, he wants us to flourish and grow. Think about the analogy of a rose garden. The rose bush can exist with relatively little work, but it will not produce beautiful roses unless it is properly maintained. It takes pruning in due season. Water and fertilizer are required. When the flowers bloom, rather than leaving them in the garden, we remove them for all the world to enjoy. In the same way, God wants us to grow our churches and personal lives to point where his message can be enjoyed not just by us, but by the entire world. Someone wise once said, "Love is not love unless you give it away."

Being the church is about loving God more than anything else in all the world, because God first loved us. Jesus is God in the flesh. In fact, that's why we celebrate his birth each year.

"Christmas" literally comes from two words meaning "more Christ." Staying plugged in to the source of Jesus Christ ensures that we change to become more like Christ and that we become the change that our churches need not just to survive, but TO THRIVE!

HOMEWORK: READ SESSION ONE AND WRITE DOWN YOUR ANSWERS TO THE QUESTIONS FOR GROUP DISCUSSION BEFORE THE NEXT GROUP SESSION

www.RebuildBook.com

SECTION ONE:
FOCUS ON CHURCH GROWTH

SESSION ONE
Church Leadership:
What Structure Should We Use?

●─────────────────────────────────●

OPEN THE BIBLE STUDY SESSION WITH PRAYER. ASK GOD TO BLESS YOUR TIME TOGETHER.

ANSWER THE QUESTIONS FOR GROUP DISCUSSION BELOW:

Scripture:

"If the blind lead the blind, both fall into the ditch."

- Matthew 15:14 (NIV)

Quote:

"Everything Rises and Falls with Leadership"

- Dr. John Maxwell, *21 Irrefutable Laws of Leadership*

What is the issue?

Have you ever been assigned to a committee in the church only to not know exactly what you were supposed to be doing? In most churches that I've served, I found this to be the case. In United Methodist Churches, we are a church based on committees. Individual committees meet in order to share reports with the committee chairs. The committee chairs meet in order to share their reports with the larger committee. The larger committee in turn shares the report with the higher board.

Sound exhausting? While it works for some, it can be exhausting! I asked one church I served, "Do all of your committees work?" They responded, "No, we have not met in a year." The difficulty with many churches' existing leadership structures is that they are STRUCTURES of an organization. Organizations need structure, but it seems that we have reached a tipping point of "red tape."

We live in a world that no longer values an organizational church . . . the world values an authentic relationship with Jesus Christ and the people in the church. Before members will willingly give themselves to the church in the present day, members want to know exactly what we are asking them to do. They need clarity in what we want them to do and training in how to do the job. What is the purpose of the position? How will the leadership position lead to souls saved for and growing in Jesus?

Why Is The Right Church Leadership Structure Important?

Proverbs 29:18 says, "Where there is no vision, the people perish." (KJV) Without a clear understanding of where we are going and clear boundaries, it's like the blind leading the blind. We come to the meetings, but we don't know what to do. We hold a leadership post, but it is simply a name on a piece of paper and not a position that benefits the overall ministry of the church. The problem with an organizational approach is that it can look a lot like a country club. It's a great place for comfort and having fun, but it may do little to build up the Kingdom of God. The building often becomes the priority. Ministries for evangelism and marketing are nonexistent. The children and youth receive very little monetary support even though they are the future of the church.

My wife, Erin, and I love the television show "The Amazing Race." The goal is for teams to race against each other around the world. The first one to reach the finish line wins a million dollars. Often, the team to lose is not the team that has the best plan, but rather the team that fails to execute their plan properly. It takes a good plan and good execution of the plan. Sometimes a cab driver costs the team the game because the cabbie takes them to the wrong address. Other times the team runs around aimlessly just hoping to end up in the right spot. The key to success is knowing where you are going and executing well. In the church of today, we need to know what will help people to know Jesus, prepare the proper plan to get there, and then execute the plan well.

God needs to be in our visioning and direction planning process from the very beginning in order for our churches to be successful. What happens when we invite God to the party after it has already started?

_____

_____

_____

How important is it to pray for God's guidance as we seek to establish a vision and direction for our churches?

_____

Thom Rainer, President of Lifeway Christian, once told a story about not praying when he was a pastor of local church. He said that he had the perfect plan for his church, but the plan fell flat. People did not support his vision. A lady in the church asked him, "Thom, did you pray about this before bringing it to us?" Thom sheepishly replied that he did not pray. It was a great life lesson for him.[2]

> A good leader seeks God's direction. Is there anything more important in a leader than he or she seeking God's direction? Proverbs 16:1 (NIV) says "The plans of the heart belong to man, but the answer of the tongue is from the Lord." Verse 3 adds, "Commit your work to the Lord, and your plans will be established." And verse 9, "The heart of man plans his way, but the Lord establishes his steps." A good leader seeks the Lord, commits his way to the Lord, and the Lord establishes the next steps.[3]

Instead of thinking of the church as an organization, think of it as a living organism. In an organization, rules and regulations dominate. Hell hath no fury like someone who crosses the line. We are supposed to be rigid and concise. Meetings are mandatory. We can argue it out until someone wins. On a vote, a 51% majority is acceptable. With an organism, all parts are important. Think about your skin. It is the largest organ in your body. If you

2   Rainer, Thom. Advanced Coaching with Nelson Searcy. July 2016.
3   Rhinehart, Brent. *Nine Essential Qualities of a Leader.* Crosswalk.com http://www.crosswalk.com/family/career/9-essential-qualities-of-a-godly-leader.html (accessed May 5, 2017).

cut it, you'll bleed. If you bathe it, it flourishes. We eat the right things so that our bodies will be healthy and grow. When our skin is dry and we itch, we put lotion on it to take care of it until it reaches full health once again. When it has a cancerous spot on it, with the help of a doctor, we gently remove the cancerous spot so as not to affect the remaining skin. Gentleness and care are keys in taking care of our skin.

The church should be much more like an organism than an organization. We should care for one another, doing what we can to make sure that each other flourishes and grows. When there is a need to remove a cancerous spot, rather than blowing a hole in the church, causing a church split, or closing, we should delicately deal with issues through consensus, taking care to insure the health of all involved every step of the way. Rigidity, harshness, anger, bitterness, lies, power plays, and lack of communication are the death nails of a church. When they are present, the organism can not thrive. While they may be present, the fruits of the Holy Spirit cannot prosper . . . love, joy, peace, patience, kindness, goodness, faithfulness, gentleness, and self-control (Galatians 5:22-23, NIV). The leadership structure will either directly confirm the mission of the church, or be the church's downfall. A lack of clarity or confusion in the leadership structure gives rise to dissension. Rick Warren once said, "People are down on what they are not up on."[4] It's a great quote indeed!

Consider the difference between a pew bench and human being. The pew bench represents the organization while the human being represents the organism. The pew bench is lifeless. While it supports the human being and keeps the person from falling, it cannot sustain the beauty of human life. Our physical body is

4   Hunt, Josh. "Thom Rainer's new challenge called Simple Church." www.joshhunt.com/mail167.htm (May 13, 2014).

defined by life, making our body an organism. People make up the Body of Christ.

> We have to see that the church is a life entity. It is not something formed by teaching or by organization. We cannot form, organize, or establish a church by our teachings, regardless of how spiritual they are. The church is born of life and formed of life. It is altogether an entity of life.[5]

How do you currently view your church? Is it an organization that values structure or more of a living organism that values people? How did you reach your conclusion?

_____

_____

_____

Moving forward, how can your church place a greater emphasis on the people in the pews and not just the pew benches? (See 1 Corinthians 12- The Body of Christ)

_____

_____

_____

5   Lee, Witness. "The Church Being An Organism." MinistrySamples.org.
    http://www.ministrysamples.org/excerpts/THE-CHURCH-BEING-AN-ORGANISM.HTML
    (accessed May 6, 2017).

What Can I Do to Develop the Right Leadership Structure?

1) Have a leadership structure that addresses the basics of your denomination (minimum required components).
2) Staff accordingly. Staffing is essential. The right staff member can help your ministry to grow exponentially. It is better not to have anyone than to have the wrong staff member. I recommend that staff oversee every area of the church. If lay chairs represent each area, let your staff work hand in hand with the laity so as to form a stronger team. A staff member's job is not to do all of the work of ministry within the church. Staff serve to resource and equip their laity counterparts.
3) I recommended three-year laity term limits for all members within your leadership structure. Two-year limits are even better.
4) Try to limit a member's participation to a single church committee at any given time. Allowing members to serve on every committee in the church sets them up for burnout. Allow your members to do a few tasks well as opposed to many tasks poorly.
5) Develop your leaders continually. Nothing is worse than a stagnant leader. Do not allow leaders into your structure who are not committed to your church through tithing and attendance in worship and a small group.
6) Challenge your leaders to a continually deeper level of commitment. Thom Rainer gives seven commitments to which every leader should aspire:
   1. Commit to move beyond the inward drift in our church. It does not take long for a church to lose its outward focus. It does not take a long time for the tyranny of the urgent to replace the priority of the important. It does

not take a long time for most ministries and activities to be focused inwardly instead of outwardly toward the community we serve.

2. Commit to renew your attitude. God has called us to serve in the messiness of life and people. We all can use renewal of our attitude toward others and towards our life situation.

3. Commit to become a more grateful leader. We need to turn to prayer and ask for supernatural help in focusing on all the blessings God gives us. A review of Philippians 4:8 would be helpful as well.

4. Commit to be a leader of greater faith and courage. Again, this commitment cannot be realized in our own strength and power. But we can do all things through Christ who strengthens us.

5. Commit to be the leader who realizes our family is our first line of ministry. Healthy families help to make healthy churches.

6. Commit to clear the church of clutter and activities. By clutter, I mean all the programs and events that keep our churches so busy. Often, too many activities implicitly discourage leaders from caring for their families and health and attending worship and small groups.

7. Commit to be an Acts 6:4 leader. If we are not giving focused attention to prayer and the ministry of the Word, our ministries will become human-powered rather than God-centered.[6]

8. I am adding an eighth! Commit to healthy church systems. How are you doing in your assimilation, evangelism, stewardship, worship, small groups,

6 Rainer, Thom. "Seven Commitments of Renewal Every Church Leader Should Make in the New Year." ThomRainer.com http://thomrainer.com/2016/12/seven-commitments-renewal-every-church-leader-make-new-year/ (accessed April 20, 2017).

volunteer, leadership, and strategy systems? A system is anything that saves you time, energy, and money. A healthy system can help amplify church and personal growth. Check out ChurchLeaderInsights.com for more on these systems and shed anything that does not fit within one of these systems. You'll thank me for it!

My Recommended Leadership Structure Includes:

Assimilation:

Assimilation simply defined is this: Moving a first-time guest from his initial visit to a fully-assimilated church member. It includes everything from when he first opens his car door to when he is finally ready to become a fully-engaged member.

What do people encounter when they first visit your church? Hopefully, it is the warmth of a Christian believer smiling and saying, "We are so glad that you are here!" From the parking lot to the front door greeters to the welcome that new people receive as they are sitting in the pews, how we welcome new guests determines whether or not guests and potential members will return. In as little as three seconds, a first-time guest forms an opinion about the church, often based upon the smallest details. How do you follow up with a guest after his first, second, or third visits? What do you do to get him to come back? Sadly, in most of our churches, we don't do much! If we do not follow up with a guest in the first 48 hours, the chances of him returning decreases dramatically. A friend of mine once said that each day we delay in followup with a guest leads to a 10% decrease in the likelihood that he'll return . . . that's a ten percent decrease per day! By Friday (following the Sunday he visited), there is only a 50% likelihood that you will get the guest to come back to your church.

I recommend that the Assimilation Team meet weekly, even if only for a short time, as quickly as possible after the worship service.

The Assimilation Team should weekly:

1) Review Sunday's service and areas for improvement with welcoming first-time guests (greeters, church appearance, connection cards, etc.)

2) Prep for next Sunday's services and who will help with what responsibility,

3) Follow up with guests. Give the Pastor a list of first time and repeat guests by Monday morning.

4) The Pastor should be prepared to write handwritten notes on Monday morning to first-time guests. The Pastor should write notes for up to 30 guests with minimal assistance.

5) Repeat guests should receive a letter as well. This letter may detail church activities to encourage guests to be more involved in church.

Biblical Basis for Assimilation:

Deuteronomy 10:19 (NRSV)- "You shall also love the stranger, for you were strangers in the land of Egypt."
Leviticus 19:34 (NRSV)- "The alien who resides with you shall be to you as the citizen among you; you shall love the alien as yourself, for you were aliens in the land of Egypt: I am the Lord your God."

Matthew 5:43-44 (NRSV)- "You have heard that it was said, 'you shall love your neighbor and hate your enemy'. But I say to you, love your enemy and pray for those who persecute you."

Matthew 25:40 (NRSV)- "Truly I say to you, as you did it to one of the least of my brethren you did it to me."

Romans 13:8 (NRSV)- "Owe no one anything, except to love one another; for the one who loves another has fulfilled the law."

Romans 13:10 (NRSV)- "Love does no wrong to a neighbor, therefore love is the fulfilling of the law."

Acts 10:34 (NRSV)- "Then Peter began to speak to them: 'I truly understand that God shows no partiality, but in every nation anyone who fears him and does what is right is acceptable to him'."

Revelation 21:3 (NRSV)- "And I heard a loud voice from the throne saying, 'See the home of God is among mortals. He will dwell with them as their God; they will be his peoples, and God himself will be with them'."

3 John 1:5 (NRSV)- "Beloved, you do faithfully whatever you do for the friends, even though they are strangers to you; they have testified to your love before the church. You do well to send them on in a manner worthy of God; for they began their journey for the sake of Christ, accepting no support from non-believers. Therefore we ought to support such people, so that they may become co-workers with the truth."

Luke 10:27 (NRSV)- "You shall love the Lord your God with all your heart, and all your soul, and with all your strength, and with all your mind; and your neighbor as yourself."

Hebrews 13: 1 (NRSV)- "Let mutual love continue. Do not neglect to show hospitality to strangers for by doing that some have entertained angels without knowing it."

Colossians 3:11 (NRSV)- "In that renewal there is no longer Greek and Jew, circumcised and uncircumcised, barbarian, Scythian, slave and free; but Christ is all and in all."

Matthew 25: 35 (NRSV)- "I was hungry and you gave me food, I was thirsty and you gave me drink, I was a stranger and you welcomed me."
Romans 12:13 (NRSV)- "Contribute to the needs of the saints; extend hospitality to strangers."

Love is not love until we give it away! The above Scriptures communicate that all people are important to God, and He wants us to love others as He loves them. How do the Scriptures enhance your understanding of Assimilation and the importance of helping guests become a part of the faith community?

_____

_____

_____

What happens to our churches when we do not take it upon ourselves to reach out to first time and repeat guests?

_____

_____

_____

Volunteers:

Find the spiritual gifts of your church members and then assign them to a position of leadership based on their natural gifts and graces. I recommend that leadership occur in instrumental steps. Just as the government would not trust a new recruit with the codes to the nuclear arsenal, we need to help people plug in gradually. Let newer attendees start by handing out bulletins or greeting. Then as they grow in their commitment to the church (both in attendance and financially), they can take on higher positions of leadership (such as chairman of a committee).

Do you remember the parable of the talents? Luke 16:10 (NIV) says, "He who is faithful in a very little thing is faithful also in much." The volunteer team focuses on leadership development. In other words, how do we help our new leaders know exactly what to do and provide them with the tools they need to succeed?

The Biblical Basis for Volunteering:

Hebrews 6:10 (NIV)- "God is not unjust; he will not forget your work and the love you have shown him as you have helped his people and continue to help them."

Proverbs 11:25 (NIV)- "Whoever brings blessing will be enriched, and one who waters will himself be watered."

Matthew 23:11(NIV)- "The greatest among you will be your servant."

Luke 6:38 (NIV)- "Give, and it will be given to you. A good measure, pressed down, shaken together and running over, will be poured into your lap. For with the measure you use, it will be measured to you."

Mark 10:45 (NIV)- "For even the Son of Man did not come to be served, but to serve, and to give his life as a ransom for many."

1 Peter 4:10 (NIV)- "Each one should use whatever gift he has received to serve others, faithfully administering God's grace in its various forms."[7]

---

7   "25 Bible Verses About Serving and Volunteering." Smart Church Management. https://smartchurchmanagement.com/25-bible-verses-serving-volunteering/ (accessed May 10, 2017).

Can the pastor do all of the work of ministry by himself or herself?

_____

_____

_____

Do you currently have a system in place to train your volunteers in the expectations of their leadership position? For instance, have you trained the greeters in how to greet (smile, shake hands, say hello, be friendly)?

_____

_____

_____

What forms of leadership development do you currently have in place within your church for those who take a new position of leadership?

_____

_____

_____

How can you further the cause of leadership development within your church? Remember: Growing and learning leaders lead growing churches!

_____

_____

_____

Evangelism:

The goal of evangelism is to make contact with people who might come and then get them to the point of being a first-time guest. How do we identify new prospects for the church and move them to the point of sitting in the pew on Sunday mornings? Assimilation is there to catch them once they are in the door, but how do we get them there? Often we forget that we cannot just sit in the pews and hope that new people will walk in the door.

The truth is that in our relational society of the present day, most often we'll issue invites to potential church guests via personal invitation. As many as eighty percent of new people who come to church will do so because we invited them. We should not neglect the other 20%, but 80% is huge! We meet new people through involvement in the community and loving beyond the walls of our church. Great churches also offer outreaches that are going to meet practical needs for families in the age groups that they desire in their church.

One of the best investments that we made at Lyons First United Methodist Church was to purchase a gas station and a building that used to be subdivided into law and dentist offices. We gutted the law and dentist office building and then converted it to our Missions Outreach Center. Each week people came to the thrift store, monetary assistance outreach, and food pantry to receive clothes, help with light bills, and food. But in the process, something else happened. We prayed for those who came and gave them Jesus through the words and prayer that were offered. While some of those who receive assistance came back and got involved in our church, two unintended positive side effects took place. First, the hearts of our volunteers changed. They were so incredibly blessed by their weekly encounters helping others that their blessings became contagious in the rest of the church. Sharing Jesus directly in conversation became much more commonplace. Second, people in the community began to say, "I want to be a part of a church like that!" Many of our newest members came because of the outreach offered in our Missions Outreach Center.

In Waycross, we started a new preschool that we named "Children First." It was started to reach out to children from infancy to age four. Within six months of opening its doors, it had 100 children in attendance! Multiple takeaways emerged from this ministry. We were thrilled to reach out to the community. It was wonderful to see people within our church have their children on the church property throughout the week. And it gave us a new avenue (directly and indirectly) through which to bring in new families to our church (evangelism!).

You may not know what to do, but do something! Before you begin with your action plan for evangelism, ask yourself, "What kind of people do we want within our church?" Name them and pray for them. Most of all, GO GET THEM!

In *Christianity Today*, Kevin Harney offered the following insights as to Biblical Evangelism:

Over the years, I have heard people say things like, "Serving is not evangelism. It is a great thing to do, but serving alone does not present the message of the gospel." Or, "Inviting a person to church or to a Christian concert is not evangelism. It is pre-evangelism." I have even heard people say, "Sharing your story is not enough. We must tell Jesus' story." To these comments and many others like them, I say, "I agree 100 percent!"

In the Book of Romans, the apostle Paul says, "Consequently, faith comes from hearing the message, and the message is heard through the word of Christ" (Rom. 10:17, NIV). Paul makes it clear that it is not enough just to love and care for people; we are called to communicate the life-changing message of Jesus Christ. Over the years, I have heard many variations on the statement, "Proclaim the gospel wherever you go. Use words when necessary." I understand the spirit of this quote, which has been attributed to many different historical figures, but I feel it is misleading. A more biblical version would be, "Proclaim the gospel wherever you go. Words will always be necessary." The apostle Peter puts it this way: "But in your hearts set apart Christ as Lord. Always be prepared to give an answer to everyone who asks you to give the reason for the hope that you have. But do this with gentleness and respect" (1 Peter 3:15, NIV).

There are many approaches to evangelism, but all of them include the wonderful moment when we tell the story of God's gift of salvation. When we serve someone and they ask us, "Why do you care so much?" we let them know how much God has cared for us. We articulate that God cared for us so much that he sent Jesus as a sacrifice for our sins. We tell them our service flows out of this understanding. When we invite someone to a church service or a faith-based event and they ask us, "Do you really believe all this stuff about Jesus?" we have an open door to share how we came to faith, what we believe, and how God has transformed our lives. We are given an opportunity to articulate the message of the gospel. No matter what our personal style, we all should be trained and ready to express the core message of the gospel, and we should know how to lead people to commit their lives to Jesus Christ.[8]

When was the last time you personally invited someone to your church?

_____

_____

_____

How does your church currently reach out to people who are not members of your church who may be new to town or not currently affiliated with a church at all?

_____

_____

_____

8   Harney, Kevin. "What is True Evangelism?" ChristianityToday.com.
    http://www.christianitytoday.com/biblestudies/articles/evangelism/faithcomeshearing.html
    (accessed May 10, 2017).

If you had to lead someone to Jesus Christ, what would you say? Would you pray with them?

_____

_____

_____

Google the term "Servant Evangelism." Pinterest is full of Servant Evangelism ideas. In the space below, write down five ways that your church can invest in servant evangelism BEGINNING THIS WEEK.

_____

_____

_____

Write down five ideas of how your church can invest in servant evangelism IN THE NEXT THREE MONTHS.

_____

_____

_____

Write down five ideas of how your church can invest in servant evangelism OVER THE NEXT YEAR AND STEPS YOU WILL

TAKE TO SEE THAT YOUR CHURCH COMPLETES THESE FIVE ACTION STEPS.

_____

_____

_____

Staffing:

In the secular world, it often is called the personnel committee or human relations department. In the United Methodist Church, it's called the Staff Parish Relations Committee. Probably one of the most important functions of the church come through this committee.

Among the most important staff ideals to which the committee should aspire are:

1) Staff for where you want to be and not where you are currently.
2) Staff for Character, Competency, Chemistry, and Culture. If someone possesses great character but misses competency and chemistry with the church and other staff, it's not a fit. If the person is not aware of the church culture or the demographic culture in which they are doing ministry, it may be a misfit. We are not looking for the perfect person, but we are looking for a staff member who can eventually do the job 80% as well as us.
3) Be willing to change staff if there is not an appropriate fit between the staff member and the church.

4) Don't rush into new hires just because you believe that you have to fill a position.

5) Appropriate staffing is huge, and it can be the difference between a well-oiled machine that is moving forward and a truck that is stuck in the mud. In his book *Good to Great*, Jim Collins calls it "getting the right people in the right seats on the bus."[9]

Staffing is an extension of the office of the pastor. Every church begins with a pastor and then expands to include more area appropriate staff as the church grows. Too many staff are lone rangers, choosing to conduct their own "ministry" within the church at the cost of the greater whole. Staff should coordinate their vacation schedules so that the staff take their vacations at off peak seasons within the church calendar and not when other staff are taking their vacation time. As ministries are developed, staff members should work together on scheduling. It should also be the goal of all staff to build up each other up by working together to make disciples of Jesus Christ.

Biblical Basis for Staff:

The most readily available example of staff I can think of in the Scripture is the staff of Jesus. Jesus recruited the twelve disciples. They were not exceptional, except for their desire to expand Jesus' Kingdom here on this earth.

Matthew 10:1-4 (NIV) recounts:

---

9 Collins, James C. *Good to Great: Why Some Companies Make the Leap--and Others Don't.* New York, NY: Harper Business, 2001.

"Jesus called his twelve disciples to him and gave them authority to drive out impure spirits and to heal every disease and sickness.

These are the names of the twelve apostles: first, Simon (who is called Peter) and his brother Andrew; James son of Zebedee, and his brother John; Philip and Bartholomew; Thomas and Matthew the tax collector; James son of Alphaeus, and Thaddaeus; Simon the Zealot and Judas Iscariot, who betrayed him."

Imagine if Jesus had tried to "go it alone." He might not have succeeded or would have been much less successful at accomplishing His mission. Pastors struggle with the same conundrum. They think that they can do the work more effectively if they do it by themselves. The truth is that we need the entire body to be complete. A diverse leadership team can maximize the gifts and graces contained among the team to better the whole team. Jesus used people who were tax collectors and fishermen as his staff. He used a man (Judas) who would betray Him and another man (Thomas) who doubted that it was Him when Jesus appeared after his crucifixion. They were like modern day staff members. They were all sinners, yes. But, they helped to build the Kingdom of God as Jesus saw their potential to make disciples.

Have you conducted an inventory of current staff? Do the gifts and grace of your current staff align with their ministry area? Is there a need for staff change or job description adjustment?

_____

_____

_____

When considering new staff, do the needed staff positions align with your vision and purpose for the church?

_____

_____

_____

When considering new staff, is a spiritual gifts inventory and personality test a part of the hiring process? If not, how can you implement this step to learn more about a potential new hire?

_____

_____

_____

Are your staff strong in Christian character and do they radiate the light of Jesus Christ? Are they living an ethical life that represents Jesus in all aspects? Do they represent the church well (both within the walls of the church and in the larger community)?

_____

_____

_____

Is tithing a requirement for staff in your church (it should be!)?

_____

_____

_____

Have you considered doing a staff Bible study or reading a Christian leadership book with your staff (jointly read and then discuss at staff meetings or another venue such as a periodic staff luncheon) to help create cohesion among staff?

_____

_____

_____

Stewardship:

In many churches, this is the Finance Committee. Historically, its focus is on the General Budget. The Committee members are often charged with the task of going over the financial figures with a fine-tooth comb. If a staff or lay member spends too much money, scrutiny is quick to follow. It often helps with the annual stewardship campaign in October or November of each year.

While financial accountability is important, unfortunately such an approach often misses the mark when it comes to teaching members Godly tithing from a Biblical perspective. Instead of a "give because the church needs your money" approach, we need to shift to an approach that encourages members to give because it is what God requires of all of us. A tenth is God's required tithe. Giving above one-tenth of your income is seen as sacrificial giving and an offering. We need courageous pastors who will stand in the gap and lead by example. When teaching on tithing, I always tell my people, "I will not ask you to go anywhere where I am not first willing to go." In 2009 based upon our household income, my wife and I tithed $1000 to our church each month. In 2010, we tithed $550 per month Erin became a stay-at-home mom. We shared it with our church not to brag, but to lead by example. As of 2017, our monthly tithe between the two of us was about $830 per month.

The entire goal of the Stewardship Team should be Godly tithing and Godly money management as a lifestyle. If members tithe, the rest takes care of itself! The Stewardship Team should encourage the pastor to preach on managing money God's way and to offer Bible Studies on money management at least yearly.

One caveat to the Stewardship Team (and hopefully all teams within your church!): Tithing is a prerequisite to service on the Stewardship Team.

Biblical Foundations:

Remember that God's intent for stewardship is that we give the first tenth of our income. Tithe means "tenth." That's a good deal as God allows us to keep the other 90% to do as we please. It is important that pastors tithe the full tenth. After all, how can we ask our people to do something when we are not being obedient to God?

What the Scriptures Say about Tithing:

Genesis 14:19-20 (NIV) contains mention of one of the first tithes by Abraham to God. Verse 19 begins, "and he blessed Abram, saying, 'Blessed be Abram by God Most High, Creator of heaven and earth. And praise be to God Most High, who delivered your enemies into your hand.' Then Abram gave him a tenth of everything."

After the Babylonian captivity, Nehemiah gathered the people together and reestablished the tithe as an act of worship to God. The Babylonian captivity was necessary because of the Israelites' lack of obedience to the commandments of God. Consider the last line as you read the passage. "We will not neglect the house of our God."

Nehemiah 10:35-39 (NIV)

"We also assume responsibility for bringing to the house of the Lord each year the firstfruits of our crops and of every fruit tree.

"As it is also written in the Law, we will bring the firstborn of our sons and of our cattle, of our herds and of our flocks to the house of our God, to the priests ministering there.

"Moreover, we will bring to the storerooms of the house of our God, to the priests, the first of our ground meal, of our grain offerings, of the fruit of all our trees and of our new wine and olive oil. And we will bring a tithe of our crops to the Levites, for it is the Levites who collect the tithes in all the towns where we work. A priest descended from Aaron is to accompany the Levites when they receive the tithes, and the Levites are to bring a tenth of the tithes up to the

38

house of our God, to the storerooms of the treasury. The people of Israel, including the Levites, are to bring their contributions of grain, new wine and olive oil to the storerooms, where the articles for the sanctuary and for the ministering priests, the gatekeepers and the musicians are also kept.

"We will not neglect the house of our God."

Malachai 3:10-12 (NIV) is one of the best known passages in relation to tithing. It talks about the direct relationship between tithing and blessing.

"Bring the whole tithe into the storehouse, that there may be food in my house. Test me in this," says the Lord Almighty, "and see if I will not throw open the floodgates of heaven and pour out so much blessing that there will not be room enough to store it. I will prevent pests from devouring your crops, and the vines in your fields will not drop their fruit before it is ripe," says the Lord Almighty. "Then all the nations will call you blessed, for yours will be a delightful land," says the Lord Almighty.

I encourage you to live a life of generosity in all things. In 2 Corinthians 9:6-8 (NIV), Paul instructs us, "Remember this: Whoever sows sparingly will also reap sparingly, and whoever sows generously will also reap generously. Each of you should give what you have decided in your heart to give, not reluctantly or under compulsion, for God loves a cheerful giver. And God is able to bless you abundantly, so that in all things at all times, having all that you need, you will abound in every good work."

What is your church's current financial situation? Could you use more money to build the Kingdom of Jesus Christ (the answer is YES!)?

_____

_____

_____

The requirement of tithing is very important. Pastors must tithe. Leaders should tithe. Members should tithe. What are your expectations of members and leaders within your church in regard to giving?

_____

_____

_____

Do you allow people into your leadership structure who do not give to your church (I pray you do not!)?

_____

_____

_____

If you do not tithe, how can you begin to step up to the plate? Can you start with 2% of your income as you gradually work your way up to the tithe and hopefully an offering (an offering is sacrificial giving over the tithe)?

_____

_____

_____

If you do tithe, can you be someone who can share the blessings of Almighty God within your life because you tithe? Pastors, I recommend that you are transparent about your tithing. People are much more likely to follow a leader who leads by example. Leaders and church members, I recommend that you share your testimony of your life before tithing compared to now.

_____

_____

_____

How do you currently educate your membership on the subject of Godly tithing? Is it a once a year sermon? What can you do to create an ongoing emphasis within your church that seeks to encourage giving and appreciate people once they give?

_____

_____

_____

For More on Stewardship, read:

Crown Financial (Crown.org)
James Harnish's *Earn, Save, Give*
Aubrey Malphurs and Steve Stroope's *Money Matters in Church*
Art Rainer *The Money Challenge*
Dave Ramsey and Financial Peace University
Bishop Robert Schnase's *Extravagant Generosity*
Nelson Searcy's *Maximize*
Nelson Searcy's *The Generosity Ladder*
Nelson Searcy's *The Tithing Challenge*

Community Groups Coordinator:

How do we catch people for the long term? How do we make sure that people don't slide out of the back door once they arrive at our church? The truth is that they must have a group in which they belong. Community Groups can be Sunday School Classes. Community Groups can be small groups of ten to fifteen in someone's home. Most importantly, members and potential members should be a part of a circle of friends who care for them and keep up with them.

One of the biggest problems in today's established churches is that we often do not notice that someone is missing until he is gone for four weeks or more. By the time we catch up to him, he has been saying, "I was wondering how long it was going to take for someone to notice that I haven't been to church!" Healthy churches form a new small group at least once every thirteen months. In fact, one in every five groups in our churches should be less than two years old.[10]

Beyond these truths is the truth that once a group has been formed for a time, it will not grow as quickly as a new Community Group. It's not that the group is not friendly; it's just that new members feel uncomfortable coming to an established group. Pastors cannot effectively manage 1) existing groups and 2) the need for new groups. They need help! I recommend a Community Groups staff person who manages the mantle of Community Groups. Preferably, it is someone with charisma, drive, and a pastoral heart who will want to see lives changed for the Lord. Community Groups can also be wonderful sources of addressing pastoral needs, both from the visits that group members make to fellow members and the information that they share with the Community Group Coordinator and Senior Pastor.

Community Groups should have Bible Study material that is approved by the Pastor/ Community Group Coordinator. New groups should have the approval of the Pastor, especially as it relates to picking the right leader. Remember the old saying, "Everything rises and falls with Leadership."[11] I like the idea of semester-based groups that largely follow the school calendar. When school is out, the groups are given a break as well.

One caveat is this: established Sunday School Classes will probably want to continue to meet year-round . . . and that's okay too! A second caveat: If a small group wants to meet during the summer or during a time when semester-based groups are not meeting, allow them to do so! It's not the end of the world! Some

10 McIntosh, Gary and Arn, Charles. *What Every Pastor Should Know.* Baker Publishing Group, 2013, p 100.

11 Maxwell, John. "Indispensable Qualities of a Leader."
https://www.johnmaxwell.com/store/products/The-21-Indispensable-Qualities-of-a-Leader.html (May 15, 2014).

new groups do fizzle with time, but that's okay, too. It is important to continue to offer new groups.

A Scriptural Approach to Community Groups:

> A biblical small group knows and does 1 Corinthians 12:26 (NIV), "If one member suffers, all the members suffer with it; if one member is honored, all the members rejoice with it."
>
> For high levels of connection and vulnerability to take place it's important that larger "small" groups either purposefully or organically form groups within the group. Sub-grouping (think: breaking groups of 12 into multiple groups of 3) will enhance the levels of intimacy and vulnerability. The smaller the group the more open the conversation. Some groups, especially multi-gender groups, might send men to one room and women to another room at some point during the meeting for accountability and/or prayer. For many groups, sub-group formation happens naturally among people whose chemistry sparks a relationship. Often those people will gather together separate from the meeting times. I can't help but think how this mimic's Jesus' model. He had His 12, and He had His 3.[12]

When was the last time that your church started a new Sunday School Class or small group? Is your church growing? (Church growth often correlates with small group participation; church decline often correlates with a lack of new groups and small group participation)

_____

_____

12 Howerton, Rick. "Defining Small Groups." Lifeway Christian Resources. http://www.lifeway.com/Article/defining-small-groups (accessed May 13, 2017).

When you start a new Sunday School Class or small group, do you give an expectation to the group on the front end that they should be ready to empower a new Sunday School Class or small group after 12- 18 months?

_____

_____

_____

Have you considered semester-based small groups and the benefits? (see Church Leader Insight's Small Group resource at www.churchleaderinsights.com)

_____

_____

_____

Does your church have so many activities that it makes it hard for people to participate in small groups? Consider doing a few things well as opposed to many things poorly. Many churches now favor a two pronged approach to church participation. They focus on worship and small groups.

_____

_____

_____

Disciple Plan Team (Church Strategy and Vision):

This team is responsible for overall church strategy. In other words, the yearly goals developed by this team feed into the other ministry areas. This team may be an outreach of your Administrative Board (or like council). They provide the plan of where we are going as an overall church. The big question we ask at each meeting is, "How are we doing on our Disciple Plan?" You may ask, "What is a Disciple Plan?" A Disciple Plan clearly defines your church's plan to win the lost for Jesus Christ, bring those who have strayed from the church back in, and nurture those already in the church to a deeper faith journey. I recommend that you pick a book each year for your Disciple Plan Team to read. I've used *Start This, Stop That* by Jim and Jennifer Cowart and Robert Schnase's *Five Practices of Fruitful Congregations*. Then, once everyone on the Disciple Plan Team has read the book, determine what you will do as a church campaign to further your church.

What is your plan for forward progress? I chose September of each year to do my church-wide campaign, because it worked for me. My Sunday School Classes read and discussed the book while I preached a four or five-week sermon series on the topic. Then, after the campaign, I sat down with my Disciple Plan Team to determine what our action plan would be for the next year. It incorporated the thoughts and leadings of the larger congregation. Each September and October, we came up with our plan for the following calendar year.

One year in Lyons, we knocked down a wall in between two Sunday School Classrooms to create a 900-square foot state-of-the-art nursery. Another year, we decided to focus on a personal growth plan. As a part of it, we did a Lenten Daniel Fast. The results were wonderful!

In Waycross, I held town hall meetings in the homes of various members and invited the larger congregation to attend. I asked each town hall what they loved about the church and where they saw a need for improvement. This information was invaluable! Out of these town hall meetings came the vision for the preschool and our search for a new youth director. While many of the items on our list have taken time to accomplish, it all comes back to a common goal. We want to continue to build the Kingdom of Jesus in Waycross, Georgia. When a church identifies priorities as a whole and follows up on them, progress becomes the norm and not the exception.

Scriptural Basis for a Disciple Plan (Church Strategy and Vision)

Proverbs 29: 18 (KJV)- "Where there is no vision, the people perish: but he that keepeth the law, happy is he."
Acts 2:38 (NIV)- "Peter replied, "Repent and be baptized, every one of you, in the name of Jesus Christ for the forgiveness of your sins. And you will receive the gift of the Holy Spirit."
1 Corinthians 12:4-11 (NIV)- "There are different kinds of gifts, but the same Spirit distributes them. There are different kinds of service, but the same Lord. There are different kinds of working, but in all of them and in everyone it is the same God at work. Now to each one the manifestation of the Spirit is given for the common good. To one there is given through the Spirit a message of wisdom, to another a message of knowledge by means of the same Spirit, to another faith by the same Spirit, to another gifts of

healing by that one Spirit, to another miraculous powers, to another prophecy, to another distinguishing between spirits, to another speaking in different kinds of tongues, and to still another the interpretation of tongues. All these are the work of one and the same Spirit, and he distributes them to each one, just as he determines."

Aubrey Malphurs, the professor of pastoral ministries at Dallas Theological Seminary, wrote, "Vision is essential to a church. However, unlike the values, mission, and purpose, the vision is more subject to change. It is dynamic, not static. Over time, the vision must be renewed, adapted, and adjusted to the cultural context in which the congregation lives. The change takes place only at the margins of the vision, not at its core. The core—the Great Commission—does not change. The details of the vision and the words used to convey them will change. The vision provides us with a picture of what the mission will look like as it is realized in the community."[13]

Visioning must be done the right way. Imagine asking your congregation what they want to do only for them to come up with 100 inwardly focused ideas. It would not go well for your church over the long term! Growth would not be realized and church would be more like a country club than a place to make disciples for Jesus. Now imagine that you work with your congregation to develop a vision that is outwardly focused. Allow your vision to incorporate two key elements: 1) Discipleship of those already within your church and 2) Reaching the lost for Jesus Christ. Then, we begin to see evangelism, assimilation, community groups, stewardship, volunteers, and all of the other key systems

---

13 Malphurs, Aubrey. "Developing a Vision." Christianity Today.
http://www.christianitytoday.com/pastors/2007/july-online-only/042705.html (accessed May 10, 2017).

start to take their proper shape. I encourage you to consider the resources below as you develop your church's Discipleship Plan.

Aubrey Malphurs, *Advanced Strategic Planning*
Aubrey Malphurs, *Strategic Disciple Making*
Andy Stanley, *Visioneering*
Steve Stroope, *Tribal Church*

Does your church currently have an annual visioning process?

_____

_____

_____

How can you teach your church about assimilation, evangelism, community groups, worship, and volunteer strategies that will help your church to grow?

_____

_____

_____

What would happen if a visioning process were not refined and reworked as time passes?

_____

_____

Trustees:

In the United Methodist Church, Trustees manage the building and grounds as well as certificates of deposit (CD's), endowments, borrowing money, building projects, and property acquisition. Often, this committee has a very arduous task.

The church building needs to be modern and up-to-date. It must be handicap-accessible and provide safe areas for children. It must have a worship center that is large enough to only be 70% full on an average Sunday. More than 70% capacity will lead to stifled growth. While CD's in an established church are often large in size and very hard to use, they can be an excellent source to help fund needed improvements in the short term. I led the Trustees at Lyons to use a CD for improvements. Following the completion of the project, the CD was replenished to provide a "rainy-day fund" for future needs. In Waycross, the Trustees reallocated a large amount of money to be used for capital improvements on an ongoing basis. In both cases, the upgrades to our facilities made a great difference in our ability to reach people for Christ.

When we grow as a result of the improvements, it is money well spent. New members mean more tithers. More tithers mean more money for ministry. More money for ministry means that you can reach more people for Christ and the budget "squeeze" lessens. Attracting new members requires a properly-maintained and attractive facility that speaks the language of today's young-adult population (especially those aged 24-50). It is up to the Trustees to insure that facilities are well-maintained in order for the church to grow.

Administrative Board (Church Board or Board of Deacons):

This is the body that votes on policy decisions for the church. Notice that I said "Policy Decisions" and not "Everything!" Too many procedural bodies micromanage to the detriment of the church. The Board should be permission-giving.

The goal of the Administrative Board is not to "lord over" every ministry of the church. Rather, the members of the Administrative Board should be permission-giving. When our church needed to deal with fundraisers, we created a policy though Ad Board. When we needed new check signers, Ad Board approved new check signers. Once a year, they approve the next year's General Operating Budget (minus the pastor's Salary which is approved at Charge Conference).

Allow a great deal of your lower-level decision-making to filter down to the teams directly responsible for the work. Staff should be empowered (in consultation with the Senior Pastor) to lead. While the pastor needs to know about all decisions and be able to influence decisions before they are made, much less needs to come before the Administrative Board. I recommend that the Board meets bi-monthly.

Visitation/ Hospitality Coordinator:

Established churches want to reach out beyond the walls and bring in new members who will find Jesus, but they must have someone who will continually love them. The pastor should love, but the pastor is only one person.

In year one of my ministry at Lyons Methodist, I hired a "Membership Secretary." Her job was to write postcards to those who do not come to church, send birthday and anniversary cards, and send care cards when someone was sick or hospitalized. I believe that it is one of the major reasons that our giving went up so dramatically. As people feel that the church is connected to them and that someone loves them, they are more inclined to be committed to the church in both tangible and intangible ways.

Waycross has great established visitation teams. They are laity who go out and visit frequently, especially with the sick and shut-ins. As a rule, I go see those in the hospital. Periodically, I make visits to my shut-ins and those within our assisted-living facilities. Laity are essential to visitation. The Pastor is only one person and cannot do it all.

One note: It takes an extraordinarily perky and smart person who is in the know of what's going on in the community to do this job. For me, it was money well-spent to hire this part-time position.

Summary:

The proper systems within a church enable the church to move forward much more rapidly.

Take Action:

Read the following books from Nelson Searcy:
Fusion (Assimilation)
Connect (Volunteer)
Ignite (Evangelism)
Activate (Small Groups)

At this point, some churches may be thinking, "I can't do that!" My response, "You can't afford not to do it!" Just do something. Pray and then go by the power of the Holy Spirit. Do what you can when you can. John Wesley once said, "Do all the good you can by all the means you can, in all the ways you can, in all the places you can, at all the times you can, to all the people you can, as long as ever you can."

RECEIVE PRAYER REQUESTS BEFORE JOINING IN UNISON IN THE CLOSING PRAYER:

Dear Lord, thank you for your church. Thank you that the church is not a building or a steeple, but that the church is made up of people just like me. Thank you for sending Jesus to die on the cross for my sins. Today, I give you my heart and soul as I commit to grow your church. Show me how to be a leader within my church, not out of compulsion, but out of a desire to see your church win the lost for Christ and help existing disciples fall more in love with you each day. Bless your church and move it forward in your love. In Jesus' name, AMEN.

HOMEWORK: READ SESSION TWO AND WRITE DOWN YOUR ANSWERS TO THE QUESTIONS FOR GROUP DISCUSSION BEFORE THE NEXT GROUP SESSION

www.RebuildBook.com

SESSION TWO
Church Growth:
What's Keeping My Church from Growing?

●━━━━━━━━━━━━━━━━━━━━━━━━━●

OPEN THE BIBLE STUDY SESSION WITH PRAYER. ASK
GOD TO BLESS YOUR TIME TOGETHER.

ANSWER THE QUESTIONS FOR GROUP DISCUSSION
BELOW:

Scripture:

"And I, when I am lifted up from the earth, will draw all people to
myself."

- John 12:32 (NIV)

Quote:

"I am ready to meet my Maker. Whether my Maker is prepared for
the ordeal of meeting me is another matter."

- Winston Churchill

What is the issue?

During my youth ministry days in Waycross, Georgia, from
2002-2006, we had a growing youth ministry. Under my
leadership, the church knocked down a wall in between two small
Sunday School Classes to create a larger youth room to allow more
youth in the door. I remember shortly after knocking down the
wall, the youth ministry started to grow even more. We moved

from 15 average attendance each week up to about 30. Later, at Vineville United Methodist Church, my wife and I were blessed to participate in a young adult Sunday School Class that outgrew the room in which it was meeting. Several Sundays in a row, the Sunday School Class was at capacity. Then, they started to experience an attendance roller coaster. One Sunday, it might be full. Then the next it might experience a much smaller crowd. The attendance roller coaster was due to a space barrier. People who couldn't find a seat to sit in did not return the next Sunday. To avoid this attendance issue, a larger classroom was found in which the Sunday School Class could meet. It allowed all who came to have a place and for growth to continue to take place.

It never dawned on me in those early days of ministry that space mattered so much. In fact, while I didn't realize it, I bumped up against space issues without even knowing it. In every church that I have served both as Associate and Senior Pastor, growth has created space issues. It is a good problem to have, but one that must be addressed quickly and substantially in order to continue the growth cycle. Not addressing space issues will cause church growth to plateau and eventually to decline.

The hard truth is this: If we do not have enough space for people to come worship, conduct Sunday School or a range of other meetings, they will not come back. Any space that is 70% full will not continue to grow.[14] Sometimes people may silently ask themselves if their presence is really warranted. Others may feel claustrophobic because there are so many people in the room.

On the flip side, we must also be careful not to have too big of a room. In a room that can seat 500 with only 20 in attendance, it feels like no one is there. Guests may find themselves very uncomfortable.

---

14 McIntosh, Gary and Arn, Charles. *What Every Pastor Should Know.* Baker Publishing Group, 2013, p 177.

Smaller churches hold the power to know someone more intimately and for the church family to be a like someone's real family. But, many first-time guests like the feeling of anonymity that a larger church can afford. They want to be greeted and welcomed, but they also do not want to be singled out. Guests like to blend in to their worship environment. Do not put a name tag on them that says, "Hello, I'm a visitor." Do not make them stand up and wave at everybody during the church service as you call out their name. Most importantly, let any recognition that you give to them be done in a quiet and private manner. Connection cards are a great way to receive a guests information as everyone at the service fills out a connection card. I also like the idea of a resource table located in the lobby of the worship space so that guests can come find out more about the church and receive free resources if they choose to do so.

How is your church currently dealing with space issues? Have you inventoried your Sunday morning worship, Sunday School classes, and small groups to see if the room size is adequate? (Remember, if over 70% of the seats are occupied, it will not grow!)

_____

_____

_____

Where do guests sit most often in church services, Sunday School classes, and small groups? (More than likely, there is a section most guests will naturally find attractive.)

_____

What steps do you take to make guests feel welcome (without attracting attention to them) in the immediacy of their first visit? What resources will you place in the hands of a guest to tell them about your church and its ministries?
ale

Christianity's Survival is at Stake

More than ever before, the church needs to grow. It needs to grow so that others can come to faith in Jesus Christ. Out of the current world population of 7 billion people, only 2 billion are Christian. Our very way of survival is at stake. From 1790 to 1970, the United Methodist Church grew each year by a similar percentage to the population of the United States. From 1980 through the present day, the United Methodist Church has experience double digit percentage decreases most decades while the population of the United States continues to post double digit percentage increases. In 1790, there were 58,000 Methodists. By 1960, there were 10.6 million Methodists. In 1970, two years after the Methodists and the Evangelical United Brethren churches merged to form the UMC, the church membership was 10.7 million. 10 years later, church membership had declined by 10.8 percent to 9.5 million United Methodists. By the year 2010, the UMC had declined by another 20 percent to 7.6 million members in the United States. The African United Methodist Church is growing by leaps and bounds, but mainline churches as a whole (including the UMC) continue a steep decline in the USA. There are success stories within the UMC, yes. But, there is a need to right the ship in order for our denomination and other mainline denominations to continue to survive and prosper.[15]

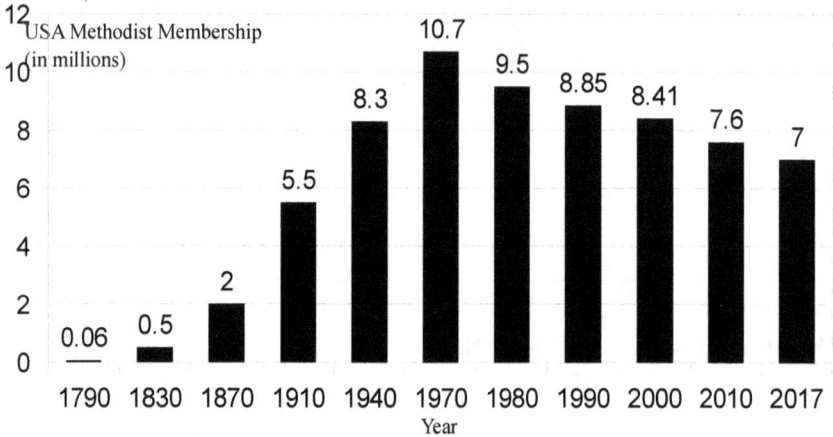

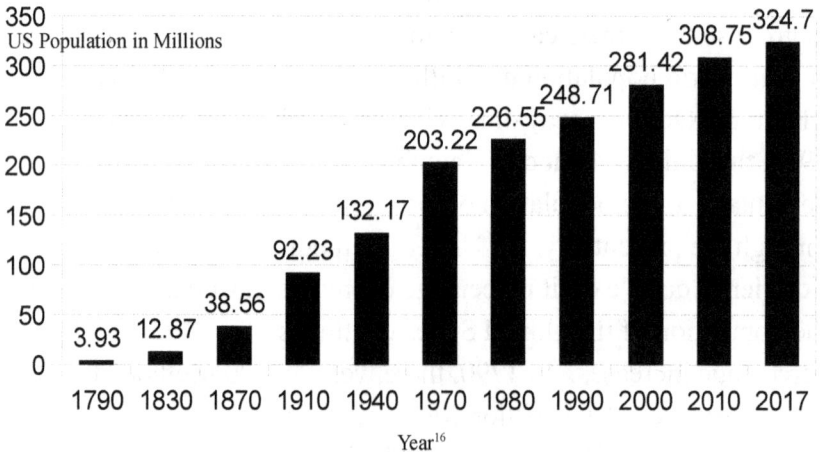

USA Methodist Membership (in millions)

Year	Membership
1790	0.06
1830	0.5
1870	2
1910	5.5
1940	8.3
1970	10.7
1980	9.5
1990	8.85
2000	8.41
2010	7.6
2017	7

US Population in Millions

Year	Population
1790	3.93
1830	12.87
1870	38.56
1910	92.23
1940	132.17
1970	203.22
1980	226.55
1990	248.71
2000	281.42
2010	308.75
2017	324.7

Year[16]

---

15 "United Methodist Membership Statistics." General Commission on Archives and History of the UMC. http://www.gcah.org/history/united-methodist-membership-statistics (accessed April 21, 2017).

16 Demographic History of the United States. https://en.wikipedia.org/wiki/Demographic_history_of_the_United_States (accessed April 27, 2017).

Churches have moved from being the center of society to being largely forgotten by those in the very towns in which they are located. More often than not, that is a sign of a lack of growth and inward focus. The populations have grown, but existing churches continue to shrink.

I remember going to Alajuela, Costa Rica in 1998. It was a great mission trip. We spent a week building children's dormitories in El Peje so that children could come to summer camp. I fell in love with the culture! I also remember getting very lost at one point during our trip with a friend of mine. We were supposed to meet the rest of the group right outside of the local Catholic Church. After about an hour of looking aimlessly on our own, we finally asked someone who spoke English for directions. They told us that all we had to do was to go down to zero on the street numbers. Dating back to colonial times, in Central and South America, the Catholic Church was at the very center of the city. It was the center of both religious and cultural life. Everything revolved around faith in Christ.

While my friend and I shook our heads for a little while because the answer was so simple, it is a great reminder of a much larger principle . . . growing our churches is not only commanded by Jesus, but it is essential to insuring Christianity has a hope and a future.

How do you feel as you see that the population has increased dramatically but Christianity in America is in a state of decline?

_____

_____

_____

What steps can THE CHURCH take to reverse the trend?

_____

_____

_____

What steps can YOU take to reverse the trend?

_____

_____

_____

What steps can Christianity take to re-establish itself as the center of society?

_____

_____

_____

What Can I do to Help My Church Grow?

Address space issues. I envy John Wesley and John Whitefield because they often preached in tent meetings. If you look at pictures of these meetings back in the 1700's and 1800's in colonial America, they were often out under the trees with no covering at all. People would come from miles around to participate in camp meetings. It did not matter if there were 200 or 2000 because there were no church walls to limit participation and box people in.

While the histories do not often record this, I hypothesize that one of the great limiting factors in the Church of England and European Christianity in the 1700's became the use of church buildings and the confining spaces found in them. Early preachers in American Methodism in the late 1700's often were known as "Circuit Riders." They did not have a building in which to worship. They had a horse. They had a list of places in which they were to preach, often preaching over 300 sermons per year.

Large tent meetings remained customary in America through the 1950's. In fact, Billy Graham came to know Jesus at a tent revival of Mordecai Ham on November 1, 1934. Billy would go on to lead some of the largest tent revivals himself such as the one in Los Angeles in 1949. By the end, 350,000 people had attended and 3,000 decisions were made for Jesus Christ. Billy continued to conduct crusades throughout his ministry in the largest available venues so that he could reach the maximum number of people for Christ. I remember my grandparents trying to attend a crusade in Tallahassee, Florida, many years ago. Apparently, they could not get tickets, so they were escorted outside. As they were leaving, the hallway came close to Billy Graham's place on the stage. They always remarked at how close they came to Billy. Space was an issue, even for the great Billy Graham! Imagine if he had chosen to do the majority of his ministry in churches that held only 300 or 400 people. His impact would be great, but it became exponentially greater as he addressed his space issues.

Google "Methodist Circuit Riders" and "Tent Revivals"? What insights did you find as a result of your search? How can some of these ideas be implemented in your church without necessarily putting a big circus tent up on the back lawn (Who knows? Maybe you will want to put a tent on the back lawn!)?

_____

_____

_____

When I first came to Lyons First United Methodist, one immediate priority was addressing space issues. The seniors had the largest Sunday School Classroom. The children met in a room that held about 15 comfortably. The nursery at the time held 4-5 babies and toddlers comfortably. During my time in Lyons, we asked the senior adult Sunday School to move to a new location so that the children could have the larger space. Because it was done in the context of helping grow the church and lifting up the children (the church's future), the senior adults graciously agreed. The children renovated the area and now have a wonderfully spacious location in which to meet. In 2013, we tore down a wall in between the old children's room and another Sunday School Class and created a 900-square foot nursery. The nursery is no longer a combined space for babies and toddlers. A divided space easily accommodates babies in one side and toddlers in the other.

The other interesting issue that we confronted at Lyons was found in the Sanctuary. The church boasts a large balcony and choir loft, but these do not count in seating space available to visitors. Visitors will sit in the lower area, but not in the balcony or choir loft (sounds logical, doesn't it?). In Lyons, about 240 can be comfortably seated in the lower seating area. Take 70% of 240 available seats, and you come up with 168. The church's average worship attendance for several years during the early 2000's was . . . wait for it . . . 168! They hit a space issue and did not know it!

In Waycross, the majority of our space issues centered around growing Sunday School classes. They were completely full! While we praise God for the good problem, we quickly came to realize that we had to shuffle the deck, so to speak. Most churches do have some available space if they commit to moving classes around to the correctly-sized spaces. Unfortunately in most churches, classes are entrenched in their existing spaces. Delicate conversations about the need to continue to grow the kingdom of God can help people to find a willingness to move to a new space. Be sure to value everyone's opinions in the process and discussions.

Space issues are important. As a parent, imagine dropping off your infant in the nursery only to see that 3 year-olds are running around in the same space. It does not make a good first impression! Parents want to know that the facilities are adequate and that their children will be safe. If these two conditions are not met, a visiting family may not return to your church. In the same way, if someone goes to a crowded Sunday School Class or overly-crowded Sanctuary, they may not return.

Whether it be knocking down walls or building, space must exist for new people to come in, or they will find some place else in which to worship. Some of this need can be addressed through multiple worship services in one worship center or multisite worship. Multisite worship is becoming much more common place in today's church and is a great way to extend your church's reach without overextended through a capital campaign. Capital campaigns have their place, but I am a big proponent of maximizing other available options first. Members should never assume that guests will naturally "adapt" to their existing setup.

We must adapt to guests and what they desire . . . not the other way around.

Summary:

We must address space issues in order to grow our churches.

Take Action:

Evaluate existing spaces (parking lot, sanctuary, and meeting rooms). Determine where you are over 70% capacity and adjust accordingly.

For more:

1) Check Out Nelson Searcy's "Barriers to Church Growth" on www.ChurchLeaderInsights.com
2) Check out Thom Rainer's article entitled "Seven Internal Barriers to Church Growth" on http://thomrainer.com/2015/08/seven-internal-barriers-to-growth-in-a-church/
3) Read *What Every Pastor Should Know* by Gary McIntosh and Charles Arn.

RECEIVE PRAYER REQUESTS BEFORE JOINING IN UNISON IN THE CLOSING PRAYER:

Dear Lord, thank you for today. We rejoice in our relationship with you. Give us the strength to take inventory of our church and to figure out where we need to increase space to ensure church growth. Give us a heart for bringing in those currently not a part of our church family. Help us to reverse the

downward trend of Christianity in our world by winning souls for Jesus . . . one person at a time. Put a boldness and confidence within our hearts and souls to bring in the lost and those who are not churched. Thank you for loving us and for cross of Christ. In Jesus' name, AMEN.

HOMEWORK: READ SESSION THREE AND WRITE DOWN YOUR ANSWERS TO THE QUESTIONS FOR GROUP DISCUSSION BEFORE THE NEXT GROUP SESSION

www.RebuildBook.com

SESSION THREE
Church Growth:
The Roles of Visibility,
Safety, and Community Involvement

OPEN THE BIBLE STUDY SESSION WITH PRAYER. ASK GOD TO BLESS YOUR TIME TOGETHER.

ANSWER THE QUESTIONS FOR GROUP DISCUSSION BELOW:

Scripture:

"You are the light of the world. A city set on a hill cannot be hidden. Nor do people light a lamp and put it under a basket, but on a stand, and it gives light to all in the house. In the same way, let your light shine before others, so that they may see your good works and give glory to your Father who is in heaven."

- Matthew 5:14-16 (ESV)

Quote:

"The safety of the people shall be the highest law."

- Marcus Tullius Cicero[17]

---

17 Brainy Quotes. http://www.brainyquote.com/quotes/keywords/safety.html (May 18, 2014).

What's the Issue?

One of the greatest successes that I enjoyed during my time in Lyons was the Wings of Hope Missions Outreach Center. The ministry included a Thrift Store, Monetary Assistance, and Food Pantry. When the planning stages for the new ministry kicked into high gear, many layers were considered. We knew that we wanted the building on US1 to help increase visibility to the church. At the time, a row of trees separated US1 from the side of our beautiful Sanctuary, which resembled an upside-down ark. People would often ride by on US1 and miss the church that was less than 200 feet away. We knew this was a problem, as did scores of predecessors within the church. Some drifters were using the fence row area to do drugs and consume alcohol. Beyond this, the 2,800 square foot law offices/ dentist office building where the Missions Outreach Center was slated to be housed had been unoccupied for 20 years and had fallen into a state of disrepair.

At the unanimous church wide vote, we approved acquisition of the property with the understanding that it would be used to enhance our missions outreach to the community once completed. The food pantry and the monetary assistance (helping with gas bills and light bills) already existed, but this would give them an enhanced ability to do ministry in a larger space. The thrift store was long a vision of the church even though no place existed to put the thrift store.

What were the issues that were associated with the church's inability to experience quick church growth? I believe that there were numerous lessons contained within this case study that centered around visibility, safety, and community involvement.

Visibility

Lyons First United Methodist Church was originally established in the latter part of the 19th century. The property was given in order for people to worship who were traveling by railroad. As time passed, roads became the norm of transportation and not the railroad.

The church found themselves on the same property location where it all began. While it was historic, a need emerged to increase their visibility to keep up with the changing world around them. Increasing visibility can happen in numerous ways. Cutting down overgrown bushes, removing old fences, and revitalizing existing buildings are several great ways to do it. The structure that was two blocks from the railroad and less than one block from U.S. 1 was now much harder to find simply because passersby could not see it. It was out of sight and out of mind.

When I came to Lyons, I talked to the new youth director who was on the job just one month before I arrived. I asked her about her experiences. She said, "One of my hardest experiences came in trying to find the church when I came for my interview. I drove up and down U.S. 1 looking for the church, but I couldn't find it!" The Dublin District Superintendent at the time also had a similar experience. He shared with me that on his first visit, he could not find the Sanctuary. He then said that when he realized how close it was to U.S. 1, he felt a little embarrassed. Luckily their vigilance in looking allowed them both to find the church, but it highlights a very real problem in many of our churches today. The church may be visible to existing members and community residents. However, it is invisible to the larger world.

One of our highest priorities in the property acquisition was the demolition of the tree line between U.S. 1 and the Sanctuary. We changed our church letterhead to read, "Located at the Corner of Wesley and State (U.S. 1) Streets in Downtown Lyons, Georgia." We installed signage that pointed people to the church on the thoroughfares through town. Lyons Methodist has become one of the most beautifully visible sanctuaries around, both from existing aesthetics and increased visibility on U.S. 1.

Guests and prospects who come to your church value visibility. They value visibility in what they see from the street and the directions that are available to them when they enter the building. Having directional signs located several blocks from your church with arrows pointing them in the right direction are essential to directing guests. Adding signage to your church doors or walls help guests to find their way around your church so that if they do not immediately locate a member (which they should on Sunday mornings), they can readily know church locations for the offices, sanctuary, fellowship hall, Sunday School rooms, children's areas, and much more.

Physically visible churches with good signage are ultra important to bringing in those who need to know Jesus. Without making an effort, guests may not know that they can meet the living God less than 200 feet away from where they currently are standing or driving!

I encourage you to increase church visibility through the occasional radio advertisement, television commercial, direct mail piece, billboard, newpaper advertisement, and other advertising mediums.

As a part of your evangelism efforts, I encourage you to do all you can to invite the outside community into your church. Handing out water bottles with a church invite or doing a gas-buy down can be great ways to reach out. You can Google the term "Christian servant evangelism" or look it up on Pinterest. The results will astound you!

Focus on increasing your church's visibility. It is essential to bringing those in who need Christ. Some people will come because they disconnected from a church long ago. Others will come who have never had a connection to a church. All need the Jesus that we are blessed to know!

Is your church visible to the surrounding community? Do shrubs or other buildings block your building and church signage?

_____

_____

_____

How can you plan to increase your church's visibility (both with directional signage and by removing barriers to visibility)?

_____

_____

_____

Safety

Many of our churches have an unenviable task. We are located in neighborhoods where people once walked to church. Churches were built for ease of access. Back in the horse and buggy days, a two-mile trek would be a long distance to travel. Today, cars allow people to drive to the church from 10-15 miles away without a thought for the drive. A 15-minute drive is standard in today's world. It's what we do!

Security issues exist in all of our churches on one level or another. Churches have not moved. People move. Low income people often live in higher crime areas. The churches located in horse and buggy locations in the late 1800's (where people once walked to church) are now located in many of these higher crime areas. Often the people who pass through the church may pose a threat to the worship participants.

I remember my first safety issue in Waycross in 2005. A man wandered in and out of the sanctuary during worship over several weeks. One Sunday the man brought a knife to church. When someone saw him with the knife outside, he dropped it in the flower bed and denied that it was in his possession. When confronted he said, "I'm going to burn this church to the ground!"

A few years later in Lyons, a drunk man who was in a police car chase parked his car in the church parking lot during an evening revival. The man looked for any open door to the church. He quickly entered the Sunday School wing and hid in an adult Sunday School classroom. I sat in the back of the sanctuary as the revival preacher gave a great sermon. The police came and talked to me. They told me about the man and the need to search our church. I asked one officer to go to the church nursery and the other to begin the search. A few moments later, the man was discovered in the Sunday School classroom and was arrested. Those in worship did not know what was going on until they walked out past the man laying in the church hallway in handcuffs with police officers standing over him.

This poses a huge dilemma . . . how do we shepherd and protect the flock at the same time? We want our churches to have "Open Hearts, Open Minds, and Open Doors" (the long time theme of the UMC), but the reality is that we cannot always open our doors to every single person who wants to attend. Sometimes we are left with difficult decisions. Most pastors did not take a seminary class entitled "How to invite someone not to come back to your church!"

When I make a decision on whether or not someone should be in worship, I usually make it based upon safety. If I can ensure that someone does not pose a threat to other worship participants or to the children located in the nursery, the person is welcome to attend. When safety comes into question, my role as the shepherd kicks in.

We must provide as safe an environment as possible in which we care for our children. Background checks of all people who work with children are a must. A child should never be left alone in a room with one adult. Access must be limited to the children's wing so that it is harder for people to enter. Parents need access to their children at a moment's notice, but everyone else does not need the same ability to enter.

I favor security cameras in all areas where children are present. At one church I served, a parent accused an employee of improper behavior. In this situation, the video actually saved us as it clearly showed that the child was well-cared for while in our custody. It was later discovered that there was potential abuse within the family at home. The police who came to our church advised us to install cameras in areas where there was a gap in coverage. It was an expense, but one that we readily paid to protect the flock, both for the sake of our children and children's workers alike.

Think about the numerous church shootings reported around the world. We cannot allow these incidences to deter us from coming to worship or our core mission of making disciples. But we must ask ourselves, "How do we remain safe in the midst of an increasingly dangerous world?" We know that bad things happen to good people, and we cannot completely eliminate threats to our safety. We cannot allow threats to paralyze us and keep us from worshiping as God would intend. But, we can minimize threats to our safety proactively.

In Lyons, our youth knew that liquor bottles and syringes were located on the fence row next to the sanctuary. Their playground fence backed up to the property line, and often the youth would kick a ball over the fence. When they went to get their ball, they would see the evidence of drug and alcohol abuse. While it did not bother them, what would the youth parents think if they knew about the liquor bottles and syringes? In acquiring the property for the Wings of Hope Missions Outreach Center, we were able to enjoy a greater mission to the community and to safeguard existing ministries located in close proximity to the fence line.

In purchasing the property for use as a missions outreach, I now think differently about property acquisition. Instead of asking, "Can we afford to purchase this property?", I now ask, "Can we afford not to purchase the property?!"

Safety allows for God-centered worship to proceed. When safety comes into question, it quickly can affect the worship experience and who might come to our churches. If you are wondering where to get started in regards to church safety, I recommend at the end of this chapter starting with your local police department. They can conduct a walk-through. Contact other churches and find out what measures they have in place, especially as it applies to care for children and youth.

Are your children secure? Can an outsider currently walk directly into your children's area without the assistance of a child care worker? What measures will you take to protect access to your children's area?

_____

_____

_____

Do you conduct background checks on all persons who want to
work with your children?

_____

_____

_____

Do you require that two adults be present with all children at all
times while in your care?

_____

_____

_____

Are adults at least five years older than the age of your oldest
child?

_____

_____

Do you have security cameras in all areas where children are present?

_____

_____

_____

Have you canvassed the areas surrounding the church building to ensure that children and youth cannot easily access items that should be off limits (drug needles, beer bottles, etc.)?

_____

_____

_____

Have you trained your ushers in how to secure the building on Sunday mornings and at other events? Do they know how to respond if an emergency occurs (call 911 and other protocols)?

_____

_____

_____

Is your team proficient in CPR and First Aid? Do they know how to use an AED device and a fire extinguisher?

_____

_____

_____

Community Involvement

I'll never forget my first year at Vineville United Methodist Church in Macon, Georgia. I was the Associate Pastor. As with any first-year assignment, I was feeling my way in a new environment. I tried to do what I was supposed to do and not drop the ball on any priority. I remember someone telling me, "Barry, you are in charge of the Fall Festival." I was thinking, "GREAT!" (very sarcastically, of course!) It was one of the highlights of the year as Vineville United Methodist Church was very engaged in the surrounding community. Vineville is located in the Pleasant Hill neighborhood. Pleasant Hill is where many low-income residents of Macon live.

When Fall Festival came around each year, the church went to the local elementary school and handed out fliers to the children as they came out of the school. We invited them to come to the church where they participated in arts and crafts, played on inflatables, and enjoyed food. The entire production was put on by the Vineville church. For one night each October, the members of Vineville gave something back to the community. They connected with parents and children who did not go to the church. More importantly, while they invited the parents and children to come to the festival, the members were able to share Jesus and tell the participants about God's love for them.

In starting the Missions Outreach Center with the new thrift store at Lyons First United Methodist Church, two opportunities to connect with the community emerged. It gave us a platform on which to advertise our church and its ministries. Toombs County and the surrounding counties offered huge online yard sales on Facebook for people to buy and sell goods, where people sold just about anything that you can imagine.

One day I counted at least 30,000 people from the surrounding area who received our posts about the thrift store. We let people know about the store and the church behind the store. Every time that I typed a Facebook post for the online yard sale, I always said, "It's one way we try to give something back to the community." Connecting with and being involved in the larger community is hugely important not only to giving something back, but also for getting new persons in the door who need to know Jesus.

In Waycross beginning in 2015, we helped the surrounding neighborhood with yard cleanup. We called the program "Good Neighbors". In 2017, we assisted in a fire relief effort as the West Mims fires raged in the Okefenokee Swamp. While we did it because being missional fulfilled the Gospel to "help the least of these," it also helped to increase our connections and visibility to the surrounding community so that we could share the life saving message of salvation in Jesus Christ.

What does Scripture say about helping others? (see Matthew 25: 34-40)

_____

_____

Do you reach out to your community currently? If not, what are three ideas of ways your church can be actively involved in the community? How will you reach these goals?

_____

_____

_____

How have you seen community outreach projects grow your church or the churches of those who you know?

_____

_____

_____

Can we be the Church and not reach out to the surrounding community?

_____

_____

_____

Summary:

Visible churches grow. Invisible churches are forgotten. Members and those visiting must have a safe environment in which to worship. Community involvement lets you give back and share Jesus at the same time.

Evaluate Your Church:

1) Can people easily find your church? Can they easily find their way around the church building?
2) How safe is your church? Be brutally honest in your assessment. Does your facility lend itself to protecting children and youth? Is there a system in place to ensure that if an issue arises, it can be dealt with quickly and quietly while not interrupting the overall flow of worship? Are there property issues that need to be addressed for church safety to be ensured?
3) Is your church involved in the surrounding community? How can you expand your involvement in the community to give something back and share Jesus?

Take Action:

1) Church Leader Insights (www.churchleaderinsights.com) offers marketing resources. Check with them to find out more.
2) Search for Christian Servant Evangelism resources on Google, Amazon.com, Pinterest, and other websites. Look for the ones that focus on inviting new people to come to your church.
3) Serve the community through outreaches such as those found at www.ServantEvangelism.com.

4) Invite a church facilities planner to help you identify "blind spots" where you need to become more visible. Often, you can call your local police department, and they will provide this service for free.
5) Implement the ideas that a church facilities planner gives to you. It may cost, but the cost of doing nothing can be exponentially higher.

RECEIVE PRAYER REQUESTS BEFORE JOINING IN UNISON IN THE CLOSING PRAYER:

Dear Lord, thank you for our lives. Thank you loving us and sending Jesus to die on the cross for our sins. Show us how to increase our visibility with signs and removing line-of-site obstacles, how to protect our church's children, youth, and vulnerable adults, and how to reach out to our community to both share Christ and bring new people into our church family. Give us a confidence and boldness to fulfill your will for us. In Jesus' name, AMEN.

HOMEWORK: READ SESSION FOUR AND WRITE DOWN YOUR ANSWERS TO THE QUESTIONS FOR GROUP DISCUSSION BEFORE THE NEXT GROUP SESSION

www.RebuildBook.com

SESSION FOUR

Church Membership:
"What Can I Do For Jesus?"
Instead of "What Can I Get Out of Jesus?"

OPEN THE BIBLE STUDY SESSION WITH PRAYER. ASK GOD TO BLESS YOUR TIME TOGETHER.

ANSWER THE QUESTIONS FOR GROUP DISCUSSION BELOW:

Scripture:

"Each of you should use whatever gift you have received to serve others, as faithful stewards of God's grace in its various forms. If anyone speaks, they should do so as one who speaks the very words of God. If anyone serves, they should do so with the strength God provides, so that in all things God may be praised through Jesus Christ. To him be the glory and the power for ever and ever. Amen."

- 1 Peter 4:10-11 (NIV)

Quote:

"Everybody can be great . . . because anybody can serve. You don't have to have a college degree to serve. You don't have to make your subject and verb agree to serve. You only need a heart full of grace. A soul generated by love."

- Martin Luther King, Jr.[18]

---

18 Good Reads. http://www.goodreads.com/quotes/tag/service (May 18, 2014).

What's the issue?

Do you remember John Fitzgerald Kennedy's famous line, "And so, my fellow Americans: ask not what your country can do for you — ask what you can do for your country."[19]? A lesser-known line follows JFK's famous line in which he says, "My fellow citizens of the world: ask not what America will do for you, but what together we can do for the freedom of man."[20] It was written in his inaugural address of 1960 at a time when the Cold War was kicking into high gear.

Nations around the world were concerned about the impending potential for war between the former Soviet Union and the Western powers. Kennedy's point was clear: stop waiting for somebody to give something to you and take initiative. If the world and the U.S. were going to be the best they could be, it would be the best because of what we put into our country rather than what we get out of it.

This same idea applies to our churches. So often we come to church for what we get out of it rather than what we put into it. Often we take the best from several churches as opposed to being committed to one. While I truly believe that it's okay to have our membership in one church and from time to time to associate with another church, it's important for us to have a church home.

More than ever before, churches need to define what we expect from our members and how members can serve God in their church. A lack of commitment on the part of a member may be due to not knowing exactly what is expected of them. Members come and do what they think is required of them, but without ever truly knowing what they are signing up for. They know that they

---

19 John Fitzgerald Kennedy Presidential Library. http://www.jfklibrary.org/ (May 22, 2014).
20 John Fitzgerald Kennedy Presidential Library. http://www.jfklibrary.org/ (May 22, 2014).

may belong to "X" Church, but the expectations of how to serve God through membership may be very unclear.

This is true for professions of faith, attendance, tithing, and many other issues within the church. How often do people receive Jesus as their Lord and Savior within your church? Many churches cannot remember the last time a person made a decision to follow Christ. It takes being intentional. Ministers should offer the opportunity for people to receive Christ every Sunday through the sermon and prayer following the sermon. They also should offer Christ in the new members' class.

When was the last time your church invited people to make a decision to follow Jesus Christ?

_____

_____

_____

What are your church's followup steps for a new believer?

_____

_____

_____

Imagine someone joining your church who doesn't know Christ! If you do not show them how to accept Christ as their Lord and Savior, the person may be a member but not know Christ. Sharing the salvation message does not have to be a long and drawn-out process, but it should be offered. Once salvation is offered, there also needs to be a way to know someone has received Christ.

People should be offered Christ frequently. I offer them Christ in my sermons each Sunday. We place the information about how to accept Christ on our church web page. I have put the path to Christ in the books I've written and on my personal websites.

A great follow-up method for someone accepting Christ can happen through the church Connection Card provided each Sunday in worship. People can check that they made a decision on the card. Once they check the box indicating that they've made a decision for Christ, we follow up with them immediately. I also believe in the good old-fashioned altar call. While I believe that society and culture are changing to a less direct form of invitation to Jesus, we should still use every available means to bring people to Christ. Billy Graham saved millions through his altar calls in crusades occurring around the world over many decades.

How often do you expect your members to come to church?

I would recommend that you think very carefully about the cultural norms as you consider church attendance. It used to be that people would attend church several times a week and not think anything about it. Now, two times per week is the norm. That means that people will attend worship and a Bible study or small group. Given this cultural norm, it helps us to understand why people do not attend Sunday or Wednesday nights with regularity. It also can help us to understand that we have to be very careful with what we are asking of people. They will choose which event they want to attend. Too many church events or church programming can lead to diluted attendance.

What are the cornerstones of your church? In other words, on a weekly basis, if you were to make a list of all of the activities and programs you offer, how many activities and programs do you want people to attend during the average week?

_____

_____

_____

On average, if people will come to two church events per week, what two cornerstones do you want to embrace? (hopefully worship and small groups!)

_____

_____

_____

Too many activities may be a cause for concern. What weekly church activities do you need to let go of . . . not because they are not fun, but because you want to strengthen your church around the core purpose of making disciples of Jesus Christ?

_____

_____

_____

What do you expect from members in regards to tithing?

Do you discuss the Biblical standard for tithing in the new members' class and periodically from the pulpit? If not, you should not be surprised when people do not give to the church. Unlike ever before, people have thousands of options of where to send their money. Unless we teach on Stewardship and help people to understand God's intention for their money, our offering plates may remain empty. I believe that plenty of money exists to do God's work; we must help our parishioners to direct their resources as God intends.

Why is church membership important?

John MacArthur, an American pastor and author known for his internationally syndicated Christian teaching radio program *Grace to You*, says that membership is important for several reasons:

1) We submit to the spiritual leadership of God and the church to shepherd us, love us, build us up, and hold us accountable.
2) We realize that being under spiritual care is necessary for our own health and well-being.
3) We make a commitment to serve the church in which we are located.[21]

As opposed to a concert or ball game in which we are spectators enjoying a performance, we make a commitment to involvement. We move from being a spectator to being the one who is in the game. God becomes the one who watches that which we do because we love Him.

21 Grace to You. "John MacArthur on the Importance of Church Membership." http://www.gty.org/blog/B130107 (May 22, 2014).

In serving the two Sacraments of the church, we relate those who receive the Sacraments to membership. Every time that a Methodist pastor serves Holy Communion, he or she stands up and says, "This is not a United Methodist table, this is the Lord's table, and I invite you to come." In saying those words, the pastor is making Communion available to all persons who profess faith in Jesus Christ. It's not because of who we are by ourselves. Rather, it's because we are a member of the Church and we need Jesus to be complete. Taking United Methodist Communion is not dependent on membership in the Methodist Church, but it is dependent on professing an abiding faith in Jesus.

Methodists believe that babies and adults alike may be baptized. The most frequent question I get is this, "If a baby cannot profess his faith and accept Jesus, then why do you baptize him?" The answer for us Methodists is simple, "We are promising the baby into the arms of God who loves him until the age when he can accept Jesus for himself." The local church commits itself to helping nurture the baby and parents in the faith until the baby one day accepts Jesus for himself. Baptism is a sign of one's new life in Christ. Someone who wants to be a member must be baptized in order to join the church. Methodists baptize by either sprinkling, pouring water over the hair, or immersion. As an infant, one becomes a baptized member of the local church. As an adult, someone professes his belief in Jesus as Lord and Savior and becomes a professing member. He is baptized and can immediately join the church if he is ready to uplift the requirements of membership. I've done both adult and infant baptisms, and there is no greater celebration both in heaven and on earth than when we baptize! Just like a birthday, it is truly a day to celebrate!

What should be some of the base expectations for members/ a new members' class?

1)

      The pastor/ class leader will share what it means to be a follower of Jesus. Romans 10:9-10 says, " If you declare with your mouth, 'Jesus is Lord,' and believe in your heart that God raised him from the dead, you will be saved. For it is with your heart that you believe and are justified, and it is with your mouth that you profess your faith and are saved. " (NIV)

2)

      The pastor/ class leader will help class members to know their testimony. A testimony, simply defined, is how Jesus helps us through ordinary and extraordinary circumstances we encounter in our lives. While it can be used at the same time that we tell someone how to become a Christian, it also can be used to encourage an existing believer. Erin and I lost a baby in 2008 and again in 2017. They were our first and fifth pregnancies. We now share how God was our strength in the midst of two difficult times because it helps others who miscarry to find strength. Erin and I pray often with others for God's comfort and peace, because we can relate to their situation.

3)

      Tithing: 10% is what God requires. Malachi 3:10 says, "Bring the whole tithe into the storehouse, that there may be food in my house. Test me in this," says the Lord Almighty, "and see if I will not throw open the floodgates of heaven and pour out so much blessing that there will not be room enough to store it." (NIV) Above 10% is our offering.

4)

Attendance in Worship: Worship is our avenue through which to uplift and praise God because He is worthy of our "worth-ship." Deuteronomy 6:13 says, "Fear Yahweh your God, worship Him, and take your oaths in His name." (Holman Christian Standard)

5)

Participation in a small group: be it Sunday School or a home small group, small groups are where the magic happens within a church. A group of 10-15 people share Bible Study and life together. They care for each other and nurture each other. They become family. Proverbs 27:17 says, "As iron sharpens iron, so one person sharpens another." (NIV) Dr. Elmer Towns shared at a workshop that I recently attended that the largest church in the world (750,000 people) is formed through small groups. WOW!

6)

Evangelism: How do you reach new persons for Jesus Christ on a personal level? Teach your new members how to share Jesus! Matthew 28:19, "Go and make disciples" (NIV)

7)

Service: Allow them to serve, but do not overwhelm. Find out their spiritual gifts and match their spiritual gifts to available areas of service within the local church. Psalms 100:2, "Serve the Lord with gladness" (NIV)

8)

Missions Outreach: At least annually, encourage your members to participate in some sort of missions outreach opportunity. This may be a mission trip with their small group, a day of service by the church within the community, or a long-term mission trip of one to two weeks. The message is simple: Being missional is important! Matthew 25:34-36, 40 says, "Come, you that are blessed by my Father, inherit the kingdom prepared for you from the foundation of the world; for I was hungry and you gave me food, I was thirsty and you gave me something to drink, I was a stranger and you welcomed me, I was naked and you gave me clothing, I was sick and you took care of me, I was in prison and you visited me. Truly I tell you, just as you did it to one of the least of these who are members of my family, you did it to me." (NRSV)

9)

Other areas for involvement: This is the church's chance to shine. What is your church currently doing to win souls for Christ? What makes your church unique from other churches?

Do you currently offer a new members' class? If so, what is taught within the class? If not, when can you start and what will you teach?

_____

_____

_____

Based on the ideas offered above, how can you make your new members' class even better? Where is there room for improvement?

_____

_____

_____

What happens when we do not emphasize church membership?

We often are afraid of emphasizing membership because we believe that increased expectations may leave people heading for the door. The exact opposite is true. When we do not tell people why they should stay and belong, they often flee. Culture is screaming for individuality and lowered expectations while people crave a raised bar. Just look at why gangs are so successful in the world today. Granted, they may be violent. But, they also give people a place where they belong with high expectations. Increased expectations lead to an increase in commitment . . . not a loss of a potential church member.

Discuss the above point . . . "Increased expectations lead to an increase in commitment." It sounds paradoxical, doesn't it? Now that you know people will respond well to increased expectations, how can you begin to integrate the ideas taught in a new members' class into other areas of your church?

_____

_____

_____

Summary:

The church should define what is means to be a church member. Existing church members should be able to attend the new members' class as well.

Take Action:

Create new member classes for your both new and existing members. Give multiple opportunities for people to attend.

Check out the following resources:

Read Thom Rainer's books *I Am a Church Member* and *I Will*.

Ezell, Rick. "How to Start A New Member Orientation Class." Lifeway Christian Resources. http://www.lifeway.com/Article/How-to-start-a-new-member-orientation-class (accessed May 13, 2017).

Garland, Dan. "Three Sample Formats for Your New Member Class." Lifeway Christian Resources. http://www.lifeway.com/Article/Sample-formats-for-your-new-member-class (accessed May 13, 2017).

RECEIVE PRAYER REQUESTS BEFORE JOINING IN UNISON IN THE CLOSING PRAYER:

Dear Lord, thank you for church membership and the blessing that comes from being a part of a faith community. As a pastor, help me to take up the mantel of teaching a new member class that will allow potential members to receive

Jesus Christ and know more about our church. I commit to teaching the expectations of church membership and helping new members plug into our church family. As a lay person, give me a heart for growing in what it means to be a true disciple of Jesus Christ as I am a member of my local church. May I support my pastor in prayer and service as the pastor seeks to gently let all church members know why we do what we do. I want to see my church grow and thrive as we all work together to make disciples of Jesus Christ. In Jesus' name, AMEN.

HOMEWORK: READ SESSION FIVE AND WRITE DOWN YOUR ANSWERS TO THE QUESTIONS FOR GROUP DISCUSSION BEFORE THE NEXT GROUP SESSION

www.RebuildBook.com

SESSION FIVE
Church Programming:
What Needs to Quietly &
Quickly Go the Way of the Dinosaur?

———————————————————

OPEN THE BIBLE STUDY SESSION WITH PRAYER. ASK
GOD TO BLESS YOUR TIME TOGETHER.

ANSWER THE QUESTIONS FOR GROUP DISCUSSION
BELOW:

Quote: "From the days of our ancestors on the savanna, we are
hardwired to add and accumulate, hoard and store. This not only
helps explain why the world is the way it is, it also lays out the real
challenge: battling our instinct."

- Matt May in *The Laws of Subtraction*

Scripture:

"He must become greater; I must become less."
- John 3:30 (ESV)

What's the Issue?

My son, Maddux, loves dinosaurs. He wants anything and
everything that has to do with a dinosaur. When he was three, he
and I went shopping together. I remember walking into the store.
I put Maddux into the shopping cart, and we began to walk around.

Without so much as a hesitation, Maddux exclaimed, "Daddy, A DINOSAUR!!!" He was so excited. He saw a dinosaur floor puzzle. It was a two-foot by four-foot floor puzzle. While I did not care for the $15 price tag, I said, "Okay son. You can have the dinosaur puzzle." Maddux found his prized possession.

What makes dinosaurs so great? Why do children love them so much? Dinosaurs were enormous. For 135 million years, they ruled the earth. If you go to Fernbank Museum in Atlanta, Dinosaur National Monument in Colorado, or the Field Museum in Chicago, you will see first-hand the enormity of these creatures. But, they could not adapt or survive. When an asteroid hit the earth 66 million years ago, a dust cloud caused the mass starvation of the entire species because vegetation could not grow. While the earth would eventually survive, dinosaurs then became extinct.

Here's the ugly truth: Whether it be the dinosaurs or the local church, we are faced with limited resources. We are limited by our money, time, and energy. If we use all of our money to pay the power bill or to pay down debt, we limit the amount of money that is available for hands-on ministry and outreach to the community. If we use all of our time on the underwater basket weaving ministry, we may not have enough time to reach out to our community. If we spend our entire day painting the church building, we may have no energy left to grow the church. God has given us limited resources with which to work, and He wants us to use them wisely.

When I first arrived at Lyons First United Methodist Church, I remember being welcomed by a drain on the church budget. I was sure that it was not intentional and that all involved in ministry meant well. However, a $317,000 budget served the 122 average worship attendance. (A wise church leader once said no more than $1,000 should exist in the budget per worship attendee). At 122 average attendance, that meant that Lyons should have a budget around $122,000. I realized quickly that we were not going to be able to increase the budget much above its current limit. We needed to do more with less. It became a matter of prioritizing. I did not take a raise the first year, but asked that the rest of my staff receive a 3% increase. We cut the existing phone bill from $350 a month down to $36, keeping three lines just like they had before. We installed more energy-efficient lighting and cut the weekly mailout bulletin down to a biweekly publication. We did a similar restructuring of the budget in Waycross. The challenge in both places was the same: Do more with less.

You may ask, "Why did you do all of this?" Simply put, we had limited resources. In the church of today, we have to come up with new and innovative ways to do ministry. In the case of the staff raises, they loved getting their raises. In both churches, we paid 100% of our South Georgia Conference apportionments each year ($40,000 my last year in Lyons and currently $53,000 in Waycross), and managed to appreciate our staff in both places. In Lyons, nobody noticed that we changed phone services. As a matter of fact, someone complimented us on less static in the lines. When we cut the bulletin down to biweekly, no push-back occurred at all. We saved an additional $3000 a year on postage and paper.

More With Less . . . With a Caveat

In both churches, saving money in one area of ministry enabled us to spend more in other areas. For the first time in the history of both churches, evangelism was able to be put into the budget. In Waycross, I also began to see the value of a marketing line item which we were able to add to the budget because of the money we saved from other areas.

As I write this, I am keenly aware that a point comes in ministry where we cannot continue to cut our budget and be successful. Many churches have cut their budgets beyond the point that they should, and now their churches are dwindling in membership, average worship attendance, and stewardship. My intent is to help churches see that often "vital" ministries and budget line items are not vital. I define a "vital" budgetary line item as being able to help us in our endeavor to grow the Kingdom of God. Growth is achieved both in its ability to increase existing membership in their commitment and love for the Lord and in the line item's ability to reach the world beyond our walls for Jesus Christ. A great need exists for all churches to define their purpose and to allow everything that they do to align around that ministry purpose. If a project or program does not align to growing those within the walls or reaching those beyond the walls with Jesus Christ, it may need to go the way of the dinosaur. Everything should point back to the core mission of making disciples for Jesus Christ.

How is your current church budget? Is there alignment around church's core vision for ministry or is the budget bloated with things that are good but do not embrace the church's vision or mission? Remember the Scripture that says, "Where your treasure is, there your heart will be also." (Matthew 6:21, NIV) Where is your treasure within your current budget? Is there alignment around making disciples and your church's vision statement?

_____

_____

Does your church currently have fruit to show for its ministry (increases in average worship attendance, increases in membership, meeting the church budget on an annual basis, and numerical growth by new believers and not just transfers in from another church)?

_____

_____

_____

Think About Your Church's Ministry Alignment This Way . . .

If something in your church is good but does not directly relate to making disciples of Jesus Christ, it should go the way of the dinosaur. It may be good, but it does not fulfill God's intended purpose for our church. While the above chart is not all-inclusive, it reveals several areas that build up God's Kingdom.

What is your church's reason for existing? Do you remember it? In Revelation 2:3-4, John records the vision God gave him. God says, "You have persevered and have endured hardships for my name, and have not grown weary. Yet I hold this against you: You have forsaken the love you had at first." It is essential that we remember our first love: Jesus Christ.

Is there anything that your church loves more than Jesus Christ? If so, how do you refocus the church's time, talents, and energy around making disciples of Jesus?

_____

_____

_____

What needs to go the way of the dinosaur?

Sometimes programs run their course only to be kept on life-support long after their lifespan is up. Are current ministries keeping you from focusing on even more that God has for you? At one time, I remember listening to Rick Warren talk about a midweek service. It was well-attended, but they eventually did away with a mid-week service in order to focus more on the weekend services.

We must continually ask ourselves what must go the way of the dinosaur? What ministries do not show fruit? Which ones are big drains on our current resources? Where can our time, energy, and money be better spent elsewhere?

Evaluate the purpose for every ministry. The purpose of the church should be to love Jesus and show others Jesus. A ministry may be good, but if it lacks purpose it should be discontinued. The dinosaurs did not get to choose when they finished their time on earth. We get to choose what goes the way of the dinosaur . . . thanks be to God!

Thom Rainer offers the following checklist in preparing to eliminate an activity or program from your church:

- Begin with prayer.
- Have a town hall meeting of the members. Share with them how busy the church has become. Get them to brainstorm and suggest activities that could be eliminated. Explain that churches can only do a few things well.
- Conduct a ruthless evaluation of your ministries with key leaders in your church. While you might not to decide to eliminate some of them, you certainly need to face with reality of what is best and what is not.
- Identify landmines. Don't step on them.
- Don't add an activity or ministry without subtracting at least one.
- Some ministries are not worth the fight and conflict to eliminate them. Focus your resources in other areas
- Have a reasonable goal on how many ministries you can eliminate in a year. Stick to it.
- The process is ongoing. Effective activities of today will be ineffective tomorrow.[22]

What needs to go the way of the dinosaur so that the energy and resources from that ministry can be used to embolden a life giving ministry elsewhere? Take an inventory.

22 Rainer, Thom. Church Answers. www.ChurchAnswers.com (accessed May 15, 2017).

_____

_____

_____

What ministries are currently not in your church that you may need to begin in order to keep your church from going the way of the dinosaur?

_____

_____

_____

Summary:

Limited resources are available to use for the Kingdom of God. We should ask ourselves, "What is the purpose of this ministry?" If the purpose is not to know Jesus and to share Jesus, we should help the ministry go the way of the dinosaur.

Take Action:

Help some of your current ministries go the way of the dinosaur so new ministries with potential to reach new followers of Jesus can thrive.

For More:

1) Rick Warren wrote *The Purpose Driven Church* many years ago, but it is still a bestseller today.
2) Jim and Jennifer Cowart's *Start This, Stop That* is another good resource.

RECEIVE PRAYER REQUESTS BEFORE JOINING IN UNISON IN THE CLOSING PRAYER:

Dear Lord, thank you for your great love for us. Thank you for your great love for your Church. Show us how to center our focus around the core principle of making disciples for Jesus Christ. Give us a passion for evaluation as we seek to further empower life giving ministries and end ministries that may be good but detract from our core mission. By the power of the Holy Spirit, create synergy that will allow all leaders to head in the direction that you have for us. We recognize that change is necessary but often difficult. We want to take the steps that will allow our church to grow and thrive in your kingdom. May that which pleases you please us. In Jesus' name, AMEN.

HOMEWORK: READ SESSION SIX AND WRITE DOWN YOUR ANSWERS TO THE QUESTIONS FOR GROUP DISCUSSION BEFORE THE NEXT GROUP SESSION

www.RebuildBook.com

SESSION SIX

Church Culture:
One Size Doesn't Always Fit All

●————————————————————●

OPEN THE BIBLE STUDY SESSION WITH PRAYER. ASK GOD TO BLESS YOUR TIME TOGETHER.

ANSWER THE QUESTIONS FOR GROUP DISCUSSION BELOW:

Scripture:

"It's who you are and the way you live that count before God. Your worship must engage your spirit in the pursuit of truth. That's the kind of people the Father is out looking for: those who are simply and honestly *themselves* before him in their worship. God is sheer being itself—Spirit. Those who worship him must do it out of their very being, their spirits, their true selves, in adoration."

- John 4:23-24 (The Message)

Quote:

"In the end, worship can never be a performance, something you're pretending or putting on. It's got to be an overflow of your heart...Worship is about getting personal with God, drawing close to God".

- Matt Redman[23]

---

23 Matt Redman. Facebook Post. https://www.facebook.com/officialmattredman (May 2, 2017).

What's the issue?

I remember as a young boy watching my grandfather, Francis Allen. He was a World War II vet who was taken captive by the Germans during the war. Later, he was the Cairo, Georgia, Postmaster during the days when everybody went to the Post Office to gather mail and find out what was going on in the world. The Post Office was the "gossip center" of many towns.

Francis Allen was a man of honor and character. I remember a funny side note to my grandfather. By middle school, I had a bigger head than the rest of humanity. I had a huge head. If a hat was not a double extra large, it would not fit! Go figure. Our genetic makeup is largely a product of traits that are passed on from one generation to the next. I began to wonder who gave me a big cranium. One day as my grandfather and I were out working on his farm in Decatur County, he took off his hat and sat it down on the table as he took a break. I picked it up and tried it on. The hat fit perfectly! It was a mystery no more. Sometimes we get big heads from our grandparents. Such was the case for me!

You may wonder, "Barry, why are you telling me this?" Here's the point: The wonderful "one size fits all" hats do not fit my head just like the "one size fits all" model for worship has its limitations as well. I appreciate the fact that most hat manufacturers have changed their slogan to "one size fits most." As we look at the church of today, we often approach it with "one size fits all" mentality. We like to let everyone wear the same-sized hat as we wear (figuratively speaking) even though churches are very different. Waycross is different from Vineville. Vineville is different from Lyons. Lyons is different than Waycross. We all worship the same Lord, but how we develop our relationship with God is unique to each content.

Take an inventory of your current community. Demographic tools are available such as PreceptGroup.com. It is vital that you identify the people in the area in which you do ministry. What insights did you gain? Are the majority of the people in your community like you or is there a mismatch between your current church offerings and the type of people in your community?

_____

_____

_____

How can your church adapt to offer ministries that will reach out to persons you currently may not be reaching? Who in your community is not being reached by any church?

_____

_____

_____

Has the culture changed within your church? Is there a need to adapt in order to bring in a younger generation?

_____

_____

_____

In Costa Rica, more than likely the people will be attracted to a festive type of Hispanic music in worship. Jamaicans may be attracted to calypso music. A friend of mine from Savannah, Georgia says that his church loves traditional worship. The same is true for Lyons and Waycross. In all three, we sing hymns and pass the plate in a very formal setting. It works for us!

Vineville was a very formal church that learned to adapt to a changing culture. They added a contemporary service in their Christian Life Center. It was successful. I came to value each Sunday as I was fortunate to enjoy worship in both contemporary (9 a.m.) and traditional (11 a.m.) settings.

Beyond the music, we face an equally great problem. In their quest for authenticity and realness, visitors and prospective members want to know how the message applies to them. We preachers often spend so much time on the theological message of a sermon that we fail to tell our people how to live it out during the week. A wise person once taught me that a sermon must have ample application. A sermon must relate back to the original context in Scripture but then apply to the person in the pew. For example, how would the message of grace apply to someone who has just lost a child? Or, how would the message of love apply to someone who has been abused? There is a constant need for us to spell out exactly how the message applies.

Bob Tuttle, retired professor at Asbury Theological Seminary, used to tell me, "Barry, tell them what you're saying and what you're not saying! It's the only way to avoid confusion!" He's right! We not only need to tell people Jesus loves them and died for their sins, but we need to make it so simple that it hits them between the eyes.

We not only need to tell people about the Holy Spirit, but we also need to give them tangible examples of how the Holy Spirit is at work to give them TODAY! An ages old story tells about a priest taking a student of his to a river bank. The priest said to his student, "I bet I can teach you very quickly how much you need God to live out your life." The student responded, "Show me!" The priest took the student down into the water and said, "Do you trust me?" to which the student replied, "Absolutely!" The priest dunked the student under the water for a few moments. The student came back up astonished and said, "Why did you do that?!" The priest dunked him again. Once again the student came back up, even more exacerbated, "What are you doing!!!?" Again, the priest dunked the student under the water. The third time the student came out of the water and exclaimed, "Are you trying to drown me?!" The priest responded, "As much as you need air to breath, you need God even more!" After the student thought for a moment, he responded, "I get it!"

Stories are great ways to make sermons applicable. People do not want to participate in anything that lacks applicability to their lives. Pastors have a hard job. We must take the call upon ourselves to be true to Scripture, but to relate it to the people sitting in the pews. If the hearer of the word does not receive the message or it is lost in translation, we need to work harder to communicate it where the hearer will receive it. If a point sounds great to us but lands flat with the people, we need to change our mode of communication.

Are the sermons in your church applicable to the people sitting in the pews? If not and you are the pastor, how can you learn more about how to relate the sermon to the person within the pew? If you are a lay person, how can you support and uplift your pastor if the sermon currently does not relate to the people within your church (In other words, how can you gently let him or her know out of love?)

How Do We Address Differences in Church Culture and Differences in Desired Types of Worship/ Church Models?

The motto of Baskin Robbins for many years has been "31 Flavors." The idea is simple: Different people like different types of ice cream. In the end, it's all ice cream! The message of Christianity never changes. The way we communicate changes rapidly in an ever-changing world. We now live in a world where technology reinvents itself within the span of 365 days (one year). That means that existing technology is now obsolete within one year! WOW!

Think of it this way. John Wesley didn't have a clue about a typewriter, computer, the internet, car, electricity, or many other modern-day conveniences. He did not have to deal with hospital incubators, modern surgery, or even medications that we take for granted in the present day. He never got caught up in rush hour traffic or at a stoplight. The ideas of High School Senior Recognition, Mother's Day, Father's Day, Halloween, and New Year's Eve took on very different meanings . . . if at all. The Gaithers were not on the scene yet meaning that Wesley never sang "He Touched Me" or some of the other hymns that we enjoy. All in all, it was a very different world!

While the sermons that Wesley preached were different in style and the songs he sang were probably written by his brother, the principles were the same. He preached about how to love the Lord our God, love our neighbor, and share the love of Jesus with others. He preached about grace and forgiveness. He understood many of the same principles that were present in the day of Jesus were just as applicable and important in his day. We may talk about the internet, traffic jams, and other modern-day conveniences, but we do so to relate Jesus to the people sitting in ways that they can understand.

We may have special Sundays to commemorate Mother's Day or Father's Day or some other season of the year, but we do so to relate a secular event to Jesus. Jesus loves mothers and fathers just like he loves those without children. Jesus loves all the people who gather in New York City just like he loves those who stay home on New Year's. Jesus wants us to be relational with those that need to know Him. Perhaps giving a Mother a rose in your church on Mother's Day technically does not directly relate Jesus to her, but if she stays for the music and sermon, the mother and her entire family may come to know Jesus then.

Walt Disney World has an ages-old principle that says, "Give the people what they want." In this case, we need to marry the world of Jesus and faith with the people who need to hear it. We need to be innovative in the ways in which we craft our sermons and music so that when people leave, they want more Jesus.

What music do the majority of people in your congregation currently listen to? Where do they work and what activities do they enjoy doing? At Vineville United Methodist, I preached to a group of doctors, lawyers, and other business professionals. At Lyons First Methodist, I preached sermons to farmers and teachers. In Waycross, I mostly preach to business and medical professionals and school teachers. While I may like my story about a tractor, it's better preached in Lyons. Stories about new and innovative technologies or a story about a surgeon in an operating room may be better received at Vineville or Waycross, because it more closely relates to the world in which they live. We need to build bridges from Jesus to where the people in our churches find themselves in the world.

What bridges does your church need to build in order to reach the people currently in the pews?

_____

_____

_____

What bridges does the church need to build in order to reach the people currently outside of your church?

_____

_____

_____

Summary:

Meet people where they find themselves in the world . . . both in music style and in sermon application. Give them Jesus.

Take Action:

Where are the disconnects in your present sermon and music styles? Where are the disconnects in your church between what is being offered and the needs that your people possess? How do we reconnect with our current worshipers and create a service that will attract new worshipers (those who don't know Christ or those who may not go to church)?

For More:

Acquire and Work Through:

Nelson Searcy's workshop entitled "Starting a Second Service" on www.ChurchLeaderInsights.com

Read:

Walt Disney World's *Be Our Guest*
Charles Arn's *How to Start a New Service*

Consider Going Multi-Site:

Thom Rainer offers several articles and podcasts on the subject of multi-Site worship through ThomRainer.com. Google them:

1) "Why Smaller Churches are Going Multi-site"
2) "Multi-Site Church for the Rest of Us- Featuring Jimmy Scroggins"
3) "Why Your Church Should Be Thinking Multi-Site"

Many churches use Nelson Searcy's book *Launch* (a church planting book) in order to start a multi-site worship experience. A second edition was recently published.

RECEIVE PRAYER REQUESTS BEFORE JOINING IN
UNISON IN THE CLOSING PRAYER:

**Dear Lord, thank you that you have created us all different
and unique. Give us the willingness to embrace each others'
unique abilities as we realize that diversity makes the whole
stronger. We pray that we may evaluate our church and find
what works and what does not. In worship styles, give us an
open-mindedness to discuss how we can improve our current
worship and potentially offer a different style of worship that
will attract people from our community to our church as we
seek to glorify your kingdom. Give us a heart for reaching the
lost and those who are not in church currently. May we speak
the worship language of our community as we seek to bring
new people into our church. In Jesus' name, AMEN.**

HOMEWORK: READ SESSION SEVEN AND WRITE DOWN
YOUR ANSWERS TO THE QUESTIONS FOR GROUP
DISCUSSION BEFORE THE NEXT GROUP SESSION

www.RebuildBook.com

SESSION SEVEN

Church Focus:
Taking Sides and Drawing Lines in the Sand:
CHURCH IS ABOUT JESUS

●————————————————●

OPEN THE BIBLE STUDY SESSION WITH PRAYER. ASK GOD TO BLESS YOUR TIME TOGETHER.

ANSWER THE QUESTIONS FOR GROUP DISCUSSION BELOW:

Scripture:

"Cast your cares on the LORD and he will sustain you; he will never let the righteous be shaken."

- Psalms 55:22 (NIV)

Quote:

"We cannot become distracted. When things appear impossible and your situation challenging, keep your eyes on Jesus and keep moving forward!"

- Bishop TD Jakes[24]

The Issue:

I remember well my first years at a new church. Under appointment in the United Methodist Church, I have experienced

---

24 Search Quotes. http://www.searchquotes.com/quotation/ (May 2, 2017).

four. In each new place, the paint was still fresh in my home and office and the people were very friendly. Honeymoons were wonderful! For the most part, everyone played well together and people praised their new preacher out in the community. In a word, being in a new location was "fun" . . . most of the time!

My first year in Lyons was a little different. The church went through a very serious issue that almost caused the church to close before I arrived. Regardless of the issue (and its outcome), it was contentious within the church, to say the least. Family members and friends were split right down the middle. Some thought that the issue should be resolved one way, while others felt that the issue should be resolved differently. The church was divided.

Within a month after arriving in Lyons, one of the pillars of the church came into my office. They said to me, "It is so unfair what they are doing!" While I will not define who "they" are and I will be careful not to identify whether the pillar was a man or a woman, you see the issue. The member was very upset, and it was their perception that someone was being treated very unfairly. The member's recourse was to seek justice for all involved.

The irony is that in seeking justice while being so emotionally charged created a toxic environment. Instead of justice being about resolution, it was about a carpet bombing. You may remember in World War II planes went out on bombing runs. The greatest workhorse was the B52 Flying Fortress. It is still in service today. Larger than a Boeing 747 (Boeing's largest plane), it can carry a huge payload of bombs. In World War II, B52's would bomb vast areas of land in the hopes that in the process of hitting a wide area. The collateral damage was massive. Homes, civilians, and churches would be hit in addition to the one target that the military was seeking.

The pillar of my church who came to me was very much like a military carpet bomber. The member meant well, but the member ended up taking out vast amounts of territory in the hopes of resolving an issue that became much more volatile.

Does this sound like a church that you know? What happens when disunity is sown within the church?

_____

_____

_____

The carpet bombing approach hit multiple targets, most of which were unintended:

1)

First, it hit at Christian unity within the church. As people did not know which "side" to take, they often would pull back from the church in many capacities. They pulled back in their giving and their attendance. "Parking lot meetings" (as I call them) became much more commonplace. People would attend various church meetings to find a resolution to church logistical issues only to go out to the parking lot and rework the issue. Some of my early meetings at Lyons had two outcomes. The first was the outcome within the church meeting. We made a great deal of wonderful progress! But then, the second was in the meeting in the parking lot. I often chased rabbits in order to ensure that the result that we came up with in the church meeting was the end result at the end of the day. Avoid parking lot meetings as they are very divisive.

2)

The second target hit by the carpet bombing was the loss of members before I arrived. I remember making several pastoral visits where former members and current members on the edge of leaving shared with me that it was just easier to start over elsewhere. They liked me and appreciated my visit, but there was too much water under the bridge. I didn't fault them for it, because I understood where they were coming from. In baseball, sometimes when a player starts in a fresh environment, he finds new life. His batting average may be higher, or his ERA may be lower. Now many former Methodists can be found at an array of area churches simply because disunity was sown over the years, and those people wanted a church environment where unity thrived. They came to church to worship Jesus, but were confronted with a very different reality in small groups, church meetings, and worship.

3)

The third target hit by the carpet bombing was the pastor. When a carpet bomber comes after the pastor, especially in the first year, it's not personal. It may feel personal and it may look personal by the ways in which it is played out. The truth is that often a member's misdirected anger projects upon the pastor. It is the pastor's job to see the forest for the trees. I remember in year one that someone said, "Oh that preacher . . . he went to Disney World with his family . . . can you believe that?!" Now I must note that I only heard about this conversation through another member friend of theirs. It's amazing how often someone will think his gossiping is in the strictest of confidence. The truth is that no gossip is ever safe! In another incident, facts that I shared in my preaching were challenged. When we added 43 members to the church and lost 60 to death by year four, I made mention of the stats from the pulpit one Sunday. The Charge Conference record backs it up. One of my members asked if I was telling the truth when I said that we added 43 members and lost 60. I could share 100 stories like these. Tearing down the pastor to build up the cause of an individual is never helpful. Pastors, while you may be tempted to lash out, DO NOT ENGAGE these types of "carpet bombing" issues. It becomes a lose-lose situation. The pastor should pray for strength and keep going forward in the good God has for the pastor's life and the pastor's church. Sometimes we need to ignore the noise.

What can I do about carpet bombers and those who sow disunity?

I pray that you never have to deal with one exactly like this in your church, because it lacks a honeymoon stage. If you do face a similar circumstance, keep your focus on Jesus! Remember that the church is for saving souls . . . as the writer of Ecclesiastes wisely said in chapter 1 verse 2, "Everything [else] is meaningless." (NIV) It is easy to take our focus off of Jesus and to put it on the situation at hand, especially defending our character when we feel it is being attacked. By even speaking a word to someone else about the negative situation, we empower the event. When the toxic member would vent about me, I often would go to a mentor outside of the church and fume, but I never spoke directly of the situation within the church or from the pulpit.

I remember saying to one mentor, "I'm so tired. What do I need to do about this situation?" The mentor responded, "Take your focus off of the negative situation and start putting it on how you are going to move this church forward." While I didn't internalize it at the time, it was probably the best advice received!

Move forward with Jesus and the negative begins to dissipate. It may not seem like it at the time, but it is true! Do you remember the age-old song that is rooted in Psalm 55:22? "Turn your eyes upon Jesus . . . and the things of earth will grow strangely dim . . . in the light of his glory and grace." (NIV) WOW!

How do we move forward?

1)

I took Jesus' side. The member who had projected their anger upon me said that it was the fault of the "other side." They wanted to know which side I was going to take. I remember clarifying my position so clearly that I surprised even myself. It had to come from God above with the help of a trusted mentor. I shared with the member, "I'm not here for you. I'm not here for the other side. I'm here for Jesus. Jesus' side is the only side that I'm on! I want to move this church forward with the love of God found in Christ Jesus." I believe that not taking the member's side caused them even more angst, but what I said got around. People started to warm up to me, and in time, they found common unity in me until they could fully put their eyes back on Jesus. I became their conduit for Jesus. When they fully realized that I was not going to take the other side, they allowed me to love them. It was an important take-away from the situation. I became a broken record, "I'm on Jesus' side . . . I'm on Jesus' side. We're moving this church forward for Jesus Christ. It's His church, not mine and not yours."

2)

I needed to take care of my family more. One of my biggest mistakes was taking it home Instead of taking it home, it would have been wise to ride around the block a few more times and sometimes to pray it out before talking to my wife about it. You've heard the epic phrase, "Leave work at work!" Well, I believe that we need to leave the negativity that often comes with ministry in our office as well. I recommend that you engage trusted friends in the ministry and your occupations as well. When an issue now arises, I call one of my trusted friends and vent immediately. Then, he gives me advice as an objective observer. It makes all of the difference in the world! You may find it important not to share current problems with your spouse until they find resolution. You may share it after it's resolved, but not in the midst of the situation. Think about it this way. Sometimes we resolve issues as quickly as they come up. If we share the problem with our spouse but not the resolution, the spouse may think there's still an issue. Our spouse is our biggest supporter and our biggest defender. They are always ready to go to war for us! It's important to learn how to let situations roll off of our shoulders and to have thicker skin . . . not because we want to be thick-headed, but because our families deserve our best and not our leftovers.

3)
      Unity is essential to moving your church forward. You may ask, "How did you have unity?" We found it at the greatest levels by having a project to work on. A handful of people within the church said to me in passing, "This church always works better when its got a project going on." What they were really saying (even though they did not know it!) was, "Preacher, when a project is going on, we all work together!" Projects can bring unity, or they can bring division. They can be the very source of life that a church needs, or they can be one more nail in the church's coffin. The trick is to find which projects a majority of the people will get behind and further the Kingdom impact of your church. Putting up video screens may seem taboo, but if you put up a grandchild's

picture, it receives acceptance much more quickly. Changing the lights in the hallways, replacing the carpet, and painting the walls may seem taboo, but if you add new members because they love how fresh and alive your church building is . . . it's money well-spent. Putting up directional signage may seem unnecessary, but if it allows a visitor or someone new to your building to find their way around . . . it's well worth it. The list is very long of what you can do, and it does not always include fixing up the building. What surrounding property if purchased can enhance your church's outreach? What missions can you participate in as a church to further develop relationships among church members? When we find common interests and focus on them, our differences fade into the background much more quickly.

4)

Pastors must identify what is directed at them and simply misdirected. I cannot tell you how many phone calls that I placed to my bosses on the District level to "cover my rear." I called them to share the situation and then to tell them what the eventual resolution might be. I remember that I would often say, "There are no action steps to be taken, I just need you know so that if someone calls you, you'll be ready." I was amazed at how many times they gave advice that helped me when I called. When people are angry, logic goes out the window. People start behaving crazy and they draw conclusions that often are not correct. I came on the scene during a very tense time for Lyons, but their anger was not about me. My job was to put the pieces back together. Sometimes it worked easily through prayer and listening. Other times, people thought I was the devil simply because I occupied the chair of a predecessor whom they loved. For the members who were bitter on both sides, it was very personal . . . especially in their dealings with me. I had to remember not to take it personally. They may intend for a bullet or barb to hit me, but I sent it on to Jesus . . . for my sake and the sake of the church. Whenever responding to a hostile person, I always smiled gently and ultimately shared with them how much God loved them. Anything beyond this would not only hurt me, it would cause the situation to escalate further. Have you heard the phrase, "Let go and let God!" ? It's especially applicable here!

5)
      Congregations need to love their pastors even more. I do not want to sound like there was no congregational love during the midst of this tense situation. In fact, there was a lot of it! Some of my best friendships while in Lyons came from people who were wonderfully supportive of my family and the ministry within the church. These people were the first to say, "Preacher, you make sure that you are taking time for your family! Preacher, I've got your back!" In fact, I know I would not have made it without these wonderful people who worked in concert with me to accomplish the will of God through the church. Thank God for faithful disciples who not only love their church, but who love their pastor and are willing to walk an extra mile with the pastor to do God's will within the church.

There is an old phrase that says, "Pick your battles." How can you pick your battles when disunity occurs within your church?

_____

_____

_____

How can you take a proactive stance in confronting people who seek to harm you or your church? How do you bring God's will into the midst of the situation?

_____

_____

_____

Sunday mornings seem to be the time people want to complain the most. I fear the moment when someone comes into my office and says, "Preacher, can I have a moment of your time?" They don't wait for my reply before they engage. How can the pastor keep his or her focus on the work of ministry when the sparks inevitably fly?

_____

_____

_____

How can you use prayer with warring factions to bring peace and unity? In a tense situation, I sometimes will simply say, "Can we pray about this issue? Let's take it to God."

_____

_____

_____

How can the pastor recruit others to help him or her to fight or (hopefully!) diffuse some of the battles that may take place within the church?

_____

_____

_____

Summary:

Congregations often take their eyes off of Jesus and put their gaze on each other. It can cause great problems! Turn your eyes and the eyes of your congregation to Jesus.

Take Action: Pastors, what conflicts to you need to let go of for the sake of the church? Congregation, what conflicts are you involved in that are unhealthy and unnecessary? How can unity thrive in your church as you all take Jesus' side?

For more: In order to move forward, often we need to turn our focus from unhealthy church dynamics to something that can make our churches healthy. Nelson Searcy's book *Healthy Systems, Healthy Church* is a good start! Research ChurchLeaderInsights.com for eight great systems on which your church can focus.

RECEIVE PRAYER REQUESTS BEFORE JOINING IN
UNISON IN THE CLOSING PRAYER:

**Dear Lord, thank you for your great love for us. We ask you to
help us as a church to keep our focus on you. Where there are
divisions, heal us and help us unite in the common bond of
Jesus Christ. Where forgiveness is needed, show us how to
forgive. In all things, let your hedge of protection be over our
church so that our members can appreciate our differences and
relate to one another as you are at the center of our lives. We
pray for our pastor, that we will support him or her with your
love as we allow him or her to lead us closer to your love each
day. In Jesus' name, AMEN.**

HOMEWORK: READ SESSION EIGHT AND WRITE DOWN
YOUR ANSWERS TO THE QUESTIONS FOR GROUP
DISCUSSION BEFORE THE NEXT GROUP SESSION

www.RebuildBook.com

SECTION TWO:
FOCUS ON PERSONAL GROWTH

SESSION EIGHT

Personal Growth:
The Importance of Bible Study and Prayer

●━━━━━━━━━━━━━━━━━━━━━━━●

OPEN THE BIBLE STUDY SESSION WITH PRAYER. ASK
GOD TO BLESS YOUR TIME TOGETHER.

ANSWER THE QUESTIONS FOR GROUP DISCUSSION
BELOW

Scripture:

"For the word of God is alive and active. Sharper than any double-
edged sword, it penetrates even to dividing soul and spirit, joints
and marrow; it judges the thoughts and attitudes of the heart."

- Hebrews 4:12 (NIV)

Quote:

"The Bible is one of the greatest blessings bestowed by God on the
children of men. It has God for its author; salvation for its end, and
truth without any mixture for its matter. It is all pure."

- John Locke[25]

---

25 Brainy Quotes.
http://www.brainyquote.com/quotes/keywords/bible.html#mdQdJ3tuGSTqU2au.99 (May 3, 2017).

The Issue:

In a recent study of Bible engagement, LifeWay Research surveyed more than 2,900 Protestant churchgoers and found that while 90 percent "desire to please and honor Jesus in all [they] do," only 19 percent personally read the Bible every day.[26] Of all pastors in America, it's estimated that only 38% read their Bibles daily for devotionals and personal study. That means that 62% of all pastors read their Bibles only to prepare for a sermon.[27] Almost 50% of Christians in the United States pray daily while another 18% say that they pray little or not at all.[28] When a husband and wife pray together daily, only 1 in 1,152 couples get divorced . . . a divorce rate of less than 1%![29]

The interesting part in the above statistics is this: When we do pray and we do read God's word, our problems are often put in their proper perspective. Did you notice? Less than 1% of couples who pray daily are divorced! That's 1%! 2 Chronicles 7:14 (NIV) says, "if my people, who are called by my name, will humble themselves and pray and seek my face and turn from their wicked ways, then I will hear from heaven, and I will forgive their sin and will heal their land."

If less than 1% of couples who pray together get divorced, how can you integrate prayer into your life as a married couple? Remember, couples who pray together stay together.

---

26 Lifeway Christian Resources. http://www.lifeway.com/Article/research-survey-bible-engagement-churchgoers (May 3, 2017).

27 Into Thy Word. http://www.intothyword.org/apps/articles/?articleid=36562 (May 4, 2017).

28 Rasmussen Reports. http://legacy.rasmussenreports.com/2005/Prayer.htm (May 4, 2017).

29 Greg and Erin Smalley; Smalley Marriage. http://www.smalleymarriage.com/resources/qa.php?catID=28&resID=14 (May 4, 2017).

_____

_____

Focus on the Family recommends the following as couples begin to pray together:

> Take the time needed to talk with each other about your thoughts and feelings about prayer and praying together. Do this without pressuring one another or trying to make the other feel guilty. See if you can agree that this is something you both want in your marriage. Talk about your fears in as open a way as possible. Talk also about your expectations up front, so they don't undermine you later on.

1. Pick a specific time and make a commitment to each other to begin praying together at that time. You'll never get started praying together on a regular basis if you don't make this definite commitment to a specific, agreed-upon time.

2. Don't be upset if you miss a day. It's important, if you miss a day, to just start again the next day. Consistency will come over time. Let yourself off the hook here.

3. Decide who will do what. For example, who decides where you will pray together? Who reminds the other that it is time to pray together? Couples reported that they couldn't just make a commitment to a time and then assume both of them would remember. It helped for one person to take on the responsibility to say, "Hey, it's time for us to pray together." It was interesting to note that for the couples who were successful, it was more often the husband who did the reminding.

4. Start where you are both comfortable. This means that if only one of you is comfortable praying out loud, then you don't start there, for both aren't comfortable at that place. If one of you insists that you pray together silently, then both can be comfortable at that place and that's where you begin.

5. Set a time limit. It was surprising how many couples made this point. "No long-winded prayers," they said. One wife wrote, "No long monologues with fourteen items in them!" Another couple suggested, "First start small and grow from there. Anyone can pattern five or ten minutes into their lives, as opposed to one hour." Another couple said, "Start with five minutes and then gradually, over time, see what happens. Don't try to take too much time as you begin."

6. Agree at the beginning that neither one of you will preach in your praying. Nothing can stop the process like using the time to pray together as a way to preach to your spouse, or to make suggestions in your prayer. Sometimes just making this a rule will give a reluctant spouse the freedom to get started, for a common fear is that one's spouse will use this time to preach rather than to pray.

7. One husband suggested: "Start with a list of things you want to pray about. This could be done individually or together. Then pray individually about your time of praying together before you actually come together for prayer."[30]

Why Bible Study and Prayer are Important:

It is a joy for Erin and me to have three beautiful children. When our first son, Maddux, was about to turn 4 years old, Santa Claus gave him a trampoline for Christmas with the condition that

30 Stoop, David and Jan. *When Couples Pray Together.* Regal Books. 2000. Focus on the Family. http://www.focusonthefamily.com/marriage/growing-together-spiritually/spiritual-intimacy/beginning-to-pray-together (accessed May 13, 2017).

we put it together. Oh, you should have seen it!!! Christmas Eve, we were out in the backyard pulling at the tight springs trying to get each of the 200 springs (or at least it seemed like it) into the right place. I pulled out my vice grips, clamps, and wrench, and off we went. We could not get the first spring to go into the right slot! After about an hour of tugging in a futile manner, we finally gave in and read the directions. As it turns out, there is a little L-shaped tool that makes it very easy to insert each spring. When we finished on the cold winter's night, we both shook our heads at how something so easy became so difficult. That's how it is in our lives when we do not read the Holy Scriptures or pray daily. We're looking for the answers and wanting to find them, but to no avail. We end up frustrated because we know that there must be a much easier way, but we just cannot figure out how to find the easier way.

How do the Scriptures unlock the doors to your life? What happens when you do not read the Scriptures or pray daily?

_____

_____

_____

Such was the case in the days of Johannes Gutenberg in the mid 1450's. At the time, only priests had access to the Scriptures due largely to the fact that it was very hard to make copies of Scripture, and few commoners knew how to read. With the invention of the printing press, Gutenberg was able to provide new copies of the Scripture in Latin much more quickly than ever before. Over time, teachers taught people how to read based on the

Bible that they now possessed. Every person who was able to read gained access to the Scriptures themselves. It began a sequence of events that led to the Protestant Reformation. In 1517, Martin Luther published the 95 Theses on the church doors of Wittenburg, Saxony, in the Holy Roman Empire.[31] By the late 1600's, the Protestant separation from the Roman Catholic church was complete.

Isn't it interesting that when the word of God was placed into the hands of ordinary Christians (and they read it!) that extraordinary things started to happen?! I do not think that it is a coincidence! People who gain access to the word of God for the first time realize just how powerful that it really is. I believe that the problem of Christians in the present day is we do not open up the Scriptures to allow them to actually work in our lives. During my time at Vineville United Methodist Church, a friend of mine who returned from a mission trip to Russia said that 75% of all Russians receive Jesus for the first time just by receiving a copy of the word of God. They read it and were saved. My friend said that it made missionaries to Russia put such a high priority on giving out the written word. Sadly, many in the United States have a Bible and can spend all the time they want reading it. Many of us just do not do it by choice . . . either purposefully and passively.

What Christian movements throughout history can you think of that were the result of fervent prayer and Scripture reading?

_____

_____

_____

_____

31 Wikipedia. http://en.wikipedia.org/wiki/Protestant_Reformation (May 4, 2017).

Think about the Russian statistic that 75% of all Christians are born again because we place the Word of God in their hands. What responsibility do we have to continue to share the Word of God around the world?

_____

_____

_____

Put into lay terms, the statistics on Bible study and prayer are alarming. As a Christian group, we read the word and pray less in a world in which we are constantly bombarded by ever-increasing problems. While laity not reading the Scripture is a shame, we are now seeing pastors who are not reading the Bible. It creates a complex that can only be described as "the blind leading the blind." Pastors cannot lead their flocks where they have not first gone in their own devotional and prayer lives. I believe that the reason laity do not heed the call to read and pray often stems from their shepherd's lack of preparation. This is true of reading Scripture, prayer, and tithing. While it is a lay person's responsibility to read Scripture and pray, pastors need to make sure that they are reading the word themselves. 100% of pastors should read the word so they can say to their flocks, "Follow me, but only as I follow Jesus!"

Consider this: "Francis of Assisi knew how to do battle with men . . . because he love to 'fly away as a bird to its nest in the mountains.' John Welsh spent eight hours out of every twenty-four in communion with God; therefore, he was equipped and armed and dared to suffer! David Brainerd rode through endless

American woods praying, and so fulfilled his ministry in a short time. John Wesley came out from his seclusion to change the face of England. Andrew Bonar did not once miss his mercy seat, and his fellowship with heaven made him the winsome Christian that he was. John Fletcher sometimes prayed all night. Adoniram Judson won Burma for Christ through unwearied prayer. Such was *the habit of those who wrought nobly for God.*"[32]

How is your Bible study and prayer life? Do you have a set time with God each day? If so, how can you continue to increase your commitment to God so that you fall more in love with Him each day? If not, how can you start to value God by a regular quiet time each day with Bible reading and prayer?

_____

_____

_____

Do you have a prayer journal where you write down your requests and then record God's answers?

_____

_____

_____

What I Can Do To Have a Better Bible Study and Prayer Life:

---

32 Cowman, L.B. *Streams in the Desert: Morning and Evening*, 365. Zondervan, 2015, p. 277.

For many years, Nike's used the catchphrase of "Just Do It." Perhaps it's some of the best advice that we can look to! Something else will constantly demand our attention . . . the key to great Bible Study and prayer is finding out what works for us. As a rule, I keep two devotionals on the console in my car. When I get into my car, they are available to remind me that I need to read my Scripture and devotion for the day. I feel like something is missing unless I have done them and done them during the early part of the day.

A personal prayer time is also important to me. I like to divide up my prayer time among various parts of the day. I pray for the day ahead on the way to work. I pray for individual circumstances as they arise. Then in the evening, I grab Erin's hand and we say our nightly prayers as a couple. She likes for me to pray. It used to bother me, but now I realize that it is not that she does not want to pray . . . it is her way of praying silently while I pray out loud.

Here are several tips that work for me on the Bible Study and prayer fronts:

1)

Don't save it for the end of the day. When we delay, often God gets our leftovers. That is not fair to us or to God. God deserves our best.

2)

Use multiple methods to study Scripture.

I personally like Audible.com. I downloaded Max McCleen's reading of the NIV Bible. I'm able to bump up the reading speed to 1.5 times normal speed. As such, I can read 4 chapters in about 15 minutes. It turns something that may seem arduous into an easy-to-do challenge. When someone asks me if I read my Scripture today, I can enthusiastically say, "Yes I did, while driving the car!" By the way, be safe while reading!

Two 365-day resources I am currently using are *Streams in the Desert* by L.B. Cowman and *Hope for Each Day* by Billy Graham. I like to hear how other people engage Scripture and Bible topics. It does not preclude me from developing what I believe, but it does add to the richness of Scripture study.

3)

A great study Bible is worth its weight in gold. Find one that is right for you. Make sure that it is rich in study-aids such as the historical setting, information on the author, what the author originally intended when he wrote the words, and so much more. When we understand where the Bible came from, it helps us to accurately apply it in the present day (and not to misapply it!). Currently, an NIV Bible that includes outlines, devotions, history, archeology, and much more. Visit a Lifeway bookstore near you and walk through the Bible section. You'll find Bibles for adults, youth, and children. A Bible is a great gift to give at Christmas.

4)

Try Bible reading plans. Sometimes I read the Bible straight through. Other times, I take a Chronological approach. Mix it up and keep it fun! And keep going! It's easy to get bogged down in Leviticus, but the Proverbs (one of my favorite books) are only a few pages away.

5)

Use devotionals, especially when it comes to your prayer life. I like prayer devotionals because they sometimes turn my routine into something new and exciting. God does not want our prayer time to be boring. After all, we are communing with the Creator of the universe who gives us the very breath that we breathe. He wants it to be fun. Andrew Murray is one good name to Google. I also like Alvin J. Vander Griend's *The Praying Church Sourcebook* as well as Patricia D. Brown's *Paths to Prayer.*

Summary:

Prayer and Bible Study are essential to our everyday lives. Without them, we lose the power to make it through small and big life events that come our way.

Take Action:

Practice several of the above approaches as you seek to take "one step up" in what you are currently doing. If you do not read or pray at all, make a small goal such as five minutes a day. If you read and pray regularly already, ask God how you can give Him even more. After all, He wants ALL of us!

For more:

Order a few of the above books and/or try the Audible way of reading the Bible. It's cool to think that you can read the Bible via audio while driving down the road! I recently visited Lifeway in Valdosta, Georgia, and noticed that they had a buy-2-get-1-free sale. I picked up a bag full of devotional books. Some I liked, others I did not like. But, it gave me a library from which to choose. Keep working at it until you find something that works for you. Never give up!

Read:

John Piper's *A Peculiar Glory: How the Christian Scriptures Reveal Their True Glory*
John Piper's *Reading the Bible Supernaturally: Seeing and Savoring the Glory of God in Scripture*

RECEIVE PRAYER REQUESTS BEFORE JOINING IN UNISON IN THE CLOSING PRAYER:

Dear Lord, thank you for the Spiritual Giants of the Christian faith who valued Bible study and prayer so strongly. They realized that a fountain of life came into their lives as they lived in your Word and prayed daily. Give us a passion for studying your Word and a thirst for talking to you as much as possible. Scripture says to pray continually and we desire to never lose contact with you. We commit to putting you first in every area of our lives. Thank you for your great love for us. In Jesus' name, AMEN.

HOMEWORK: READ SESSION NINE AND WRITE DOWN YOUR ANSWERS TO THE QUESTIONS FOR GROUP DISCUSSION BEFORE THE NEXT GROUP SESSION

www.RebuildBook.com

SESSION NINE

Personal Health:
Health as a Christian Lifestyle

———————●———————

OPEN THE BIBLE STUDY SESSION WITH PRAYER. ASK
GOD TO BLESS YOUR TIME TOGETHER.

ANSWER THE QUESTIONS FOR GROUP DISCUSSION
BELOW

Scripture:

"Do you not know that your body is a temple of the Holy Spirit
within you, which you have from God, and that you are not your
own? For you were bought with a price; therefore glorify God in
your body."

- 1Corinthians 6:19-20 (NRSV)

Quote:

"The greatest wealth is health."

- Virgil[33]

The Issue:

When I was the Associate Pastor of Waycross First United
Methodist Church from 2002-2006, I remember eating healthy for
a short time. I ate a small chicken breast cooked on the George

---

[33] Jennifer Pfeffer. "21 Healthy Lifestyle Rules to Inspire
You.".http://www.rasmussen.edu/degrees/health-sciences/blog/healthy-lifestyle-quotes-to-
inspire-you/ (May 4, 2017).

Foreman Grille along with two vegetables every night for supper. It was in response to the fact that at the time the doctor told me that I was well on the way to becoming a diabetic. My triglycerides and my bad cholesterol were hovering in the 300-500 range . . . NOT GOOD! Over time, my health got better and I eventually got off the diet. I went back to eating what I love to eat, including steaks and sugary sodas. I took the approach that it was a "one and done" type challenge.

During my time in Macon at Vineville United Methodist Church, the same issues cropped up again and again. My body was a ticking time bomb, but I largely ignored the signs of it and enjoyed a very healthy diet indeed . . . if I wanted to eat, I did! Coffee became a "prop me up" largely because by the end of the day, my body was ready to collapse. I needed some caffeine just to get me through the evening hours before bedtime.

In 2010 when I arrived at Lyons, I weighed 210 pounds. For a six-foot tall guy with a slender frame, I was about 35 pounds overweight (maybe even more!). My new doctor put me on a cholesterol medication and told me that I needed to watch the triglycerides. Even so, I continued to eat all that I desired.

In 2013 while attending the Renegade Pastors Conference in Orlando, Florida, I finally had an epiphany. With my cup of coffee in hand to make it through the evening hours, I attended Steve Reynold's workshop on his new book *Get Off the Couch*. Steve talked about Scripture as the source for weight loss. In fact, when Steve was overweight and headed down a dark road of high blood pressure, diabetes, and other conditions, God told him to go to the Scriptures for help. The result was that Steve took it upon himself to lose weight, but he also became a crusader for the cause of healthy living as it relates to Scripture.

Steve's website (www.bod4god.org) and his organization (Losing to Live) are shining examples of what it means to value our bodies within a Godly context.   During Steve's talk, he shared the story of when his first granddaughter was born. He said that it further reminded him the importance of healthy living because he wanted to be around as long as possible to help nurture his granddaughter in the faith and take care of her as she grows up. If Steve were to die prematurely, not only would it have a grave impact upon him (obviously!), but it would affect his ability to contribute to the well-being and healthy lifestyle of his children and grandchildren.

My experience with Steve combined with my experience that same weekend with Dr. Elmer Towns was the one-two punch that I needed to get my own health turned around. Dr. Towns wrote a series of books on Spiritual Breakthrough. He now has several versions of the book including one for fasting. The one in the series that I love the most is *Fasting for Spiritual Breakthrough: The Daniel Fast.*

I made a commitment to myself and God to try my best to live a more healthy Christian lifestyle. I want to be around for as long as possible so that I can influence my own family in a positive way. Beyond this, I want to make sure that I am as healthy as possible for the years that I am still on this earth. Heaven is a party, but I'm not ready to go just yet!

I began by cutting out the sugar, dairy ice cream, red meat, and fried foods. I cut out sodas all together and began to try to only put into my body what was going to have some nutritional value. I lost 21 pounds. I went from 206 pounds down to 185 pounds.

During the following Lenten Season, I challenged my church to healthy living by participating in Dr. Town's *Daniel Fast: Fasting for Spiritual Breakthrough.* It was incredible! While I thought that only a handful of people would join me in the fast, we ended up with about 50 people who took either the 10-day or

21-day fast. I was elated! I made it the full 21 days and can truly say that I feel much closer to God as a result.

For four years, I have participated in the Daniel Fast. It is not easy, and I have experienced regression. The first three years, I gained the weight back. In Pearson, Georgia, a place called "The Country Cabin" serves delicious food! It is easy to overeat instead of finding moderation. While my weight gain and loss has been a bit of roller coaster ride, it has prepared me for where I find myself today.

In my endeavor to lose weight through the Lenten Daniel Fast, I developed more willpower each year. I know that weight loss is good for me, and I do not want to die young. As of Easter 2017, I lost the annual 30 pounds. During the Lenten Daniel Fast, I made a plan for eating healthy AFTER the Lenten Fast was complete. I informed my wife that I would only eat meat such as grilled or baked chicken, fish, and turkey. I also am committed to eating no fried food and drinking water as much as possible. I am avoiding sugary beverages and keeping snacks to fruits and occasional peanut butter. Having a plan and sticking to it has been a process, but I feel like the struggle has led me to the point where I am finally following through. I am not committed to giving up The Country Cabin forever, but I need to be more careful about eating in moderation when I go.

When was the last time that you had a physical that included blood work? If so, what were the results? If not, when will you schedule an appointment to go to the doctor's office for blood work and a physical?

_____

_____

Do you eat in moderation when going out to eat? Portion control is a great part of watching your diet. Do you exercise regularly? Do you record your weight on a regular basis to get a baseline for where your weight stands on an ongoing basis?

_____

_____

_____

Do you exercise? If not, can you begin to make 10,000 steps a priority each day? Use a pedometer to keep you honest! Is there someone who can hold you accountable for your exercise?

_____

_____

_____

Why is a Healthy Christian Lifestyle Important?

1)

Scripture requires it. 1 Corinthians 6:19 says, "Do you not know that your bodies are temples of the Holy Spirit, who is in you, whom you have received from God? You are not your own." (NIV) Scripture reminds us that we are stewards of the body to which God has entrusted us. We want to do all in our power to take care of it and nurture it. We want to make sure that we put nothing into our bodies that will purposefully harm it. I love the commercial on television that shows a car with a boat anchor behind it. The car is going only about 10 miles an hour, because it cannot manage a greater speed with the huge boat anchor dragging on the highway. In the same way, if our bodies are being slowed by the harmful toxins we put into it, how can we fully allow the Holy Spirit to indwell in us? No matter how much abuse our bodies take because of a lack of care, we are never too old to start. And we live a healthy lifestyle because God deserves our best.

Your body is the temple of God. As such, what are you currently putting into the temple that is not good for you? How can you change your eating habits to more healthy food choices?

_____

_____

_____

2)
Without health, we may sit on the sidelines of life. I'm a big fan of baseball. Particularly, I love the Atlanta Braves. For a long time, the Braves were perennial winners. They would continually find ways to grind it out and to get the job done. Sometimes a player did not live up to expectations. Maybe it was their low batting average or their high pitching ERA. Sometimes, however, it was their health.

While a health condition may not publicly be blamed on too many cheeseburgers or the pitcher's inattention to physical conditioning, the results sometimes speak for themselves. When players are on the Disabled List (DL), they cannot use their talent to help their team win. In the church, when we do not take care of our bodies, we may be on the church's DL. In life, we may be on our work's DL or the family DL. In the church, we may want to help win souls for Christ, but if we are sick or in the hospital because of a preventable medical condition, we cannot help the team win. Good health is vital to winning souls for Christ and sharing Christ with our families and friends.

What current life choices could threaten to put you on the sidelines of life if you do not make a change?

_____

_____

_____

3)

Good health brings us closer to God. When I first participated in the Daniel Fast for 21 days, something beyond me happened. I felt close to God in a way that I cannot explain, as if detoxing my body caused me to have more space in my heart where God could make a home. I felt so close to God in ways that defy explanation. Giving up something created a space in which God could indwell.

Can you take on a cleansing program such as *The Daniel Fast* for both weight loss and spiritual renewal? If so, google *The Daniel Fast* and figure out a plan for when you could do it with others who might join with you. Write down your plan for moving forward.

_____

_____

_____

What Can I Do To Live a Healthy Christian Lifestyle?

Simple put, DIET AND EXERCISE. In the beginning it's not going to be easy, but it does get a lot great deal easier as good habits are developed. My body no longer craves the sweetness of sugar. My mind feels much more alert. I have much more energy at 178 pounds than I did at 210.

It's amazing how quickly our bodies can adapt, but it takes purposeful effort. Try reading Elmer Town's book *The Daniel Fast: Fasting for Spiritual Breakthrough.* Try reading Steve Reynold's resources *Bod for God* and *Get Off the Couch.* Steve also co-wrote a book with Nelson Searcy for pastors entitled *The Healthy Renegade Pastor.* Find a team of people who are willing to pray for you in the process. I've got a team of people that I know are praying for me right now, and it is making a huge difference.

Find an accountability partner who can walk through the process of weight loss and exercise with you. Hold your accountability partner accountable as well. We should not go it alone. The danger of going it alone is regaining the weight previously lost.

Take a look at my progress over the four years of doing the Daniel Fast over Lent (46 actual days). You'll notice that during the fast each year I did well. The challenge was to continue healthy habits after the fast was over. Year one, I did terrible!

With Easter came the same old eating habits, and I regressed completely to the old self. The next year, I did a little better after Easter. By year four, I was able to make the healthy decisions during the Lenten Daniel Fast that allowed me to keep the weight off after Easter. You may have a similar experience as well.

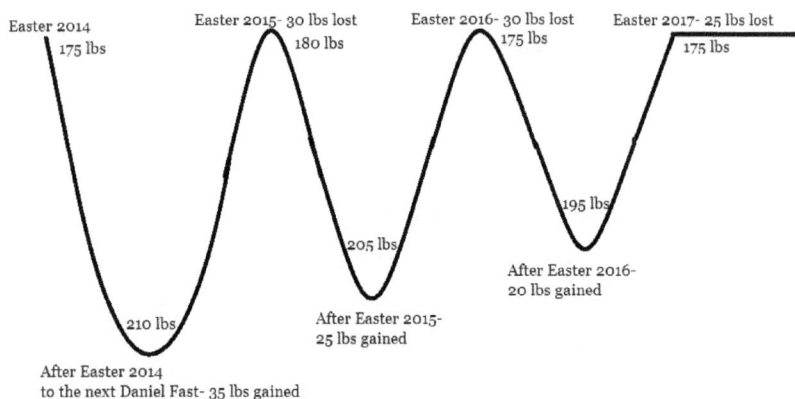

Easter 2014
175 lbs

Easter 2015- 30 lbs lost
180 lbs

Easter 2016- 30 lbs lost
175 lbs

Easter 2017- 25 lbs lost
175 lbs

205 lbs

195 lbs

After Easter 2016-
20 lbs gained

210 lbs

After Easter 2015-
25 lbs gained

After Easter 2014
to the next Daniel Fast- 35 lbs gained

Notice the above illustration. First, from Ash Wednesday 2014 to Easter 2014, I lost 30 pounds. Then, I regressed after Easter 2014. I ate like a crazy man. Each year, I gained less weight as I lost the same amount of weight, leading to overall weight loss.

Weight loss and healthy habits are a journey. No one is going to "arrive" in 40 days. If they do, question whether or not they are telling you the truth. I am not going to say that there are not exceptions, but the people are few and far between who can stop eating and start healthy habits in a day (or even a few weeks). I ate healthy growing up. From age 18 until age 38, I ate as I pleased and my body and health revealed my poor food choices. Food tastes delicious! But is it really worth sacrificing your future because you may die at a young age?

Today, I must still watch my health. I have a good body weight, but not-so-good genes. My bad cholesterol and my triglycerides are usually elevated even with my low weight.

Genetics play a large role in your health. Yearly physicals are essential because they reveal conditions that may sideline you if left untreated. We all can and should live a more healthy lifestyle. The key is to get in the game!

Summary:

A healthy body is a body that honors God. God wants to honor us as we honor Him . . . especially with our bodies.

Take Action:

What lifestyle changes do you need to make? How can you make sure that you stay in the game for the long haul?

For more:

1. All should read Dr. Elmer Town's *Fasting for Spiritual Breakthrough: The Daniel Fast.*
2) All should read and work through Steve Reynold's book *Bod for God.*
3) Men should read Steve Reynolds book *Get off the Couch.*
4) Pastors should read Nelson Searcy's and Steve Reynold's co-authored book *The Healthy Renegade Pastor.*

RECEIVE PRAYER REQUESTS BEFORE JOINING IN
UNISON IN THE CLOSING PRAYER:

**Dear Lord, thank you for your great love for me. Thank
you for the gift of food and the blessing of eating, both of
which I love! I pray that you will give me the will power to
eat all things in moderation and to not put anything into
my body that is unhealthy because my body is your temple.
Give me a heart for taking part in cleansing programs such
as *The Daniel Fast* during Lent, so that I can focus not just
on weight reduction, but also on creating a space in my life
where you can indwell. I pray that I may make exercise a
regular part of my life and get an annual physical so that I
can know more about my blood work and body. As I make
healthy life choices, may I grow in my love for you. Help
me join with others who can hold me accountable to
healthy choices as a lifestyle. In Jesus' name, AMEN.**

HOMEWORK: READ SESSION TEN AND WRITE DOWN
YOUR ANSWERS TO THE QUESTIONS FOR GROUP
DISCUSSION BEFORE THE NEXT GROUP SESSION

www.RebuildBook.com

SESSION TEN
Personal Rest:
Valuing Sabbath

●━━━━━━━━━━━━━━━━━━━━━━━━━━━●

OPEN THE BIBLE STUDY SESSION WITH PRAYER. ASK GOD TO BLESS YOUR TIME TOGETHER.

ANSWER THE QUESTIONS FOR GROUP DISCUSSION BELOW:

Scripture:

"Thus the heavens and the earth were finished, and all their multitude. And on the seventh day God finished the work that he had done, and he rested on the seventh day from all the work that he had done. So God blessed the seventh day and hallowed it, because on it God rested from all the work that he had done in creation."

- Genesis 2:1-3 (NRSV)

Short Story:

One man challenged another to an all-day wood chopping contest. The challenger worked very hard, stopping only for a brief lunch break. The other man had a leisurely lunch and took several breaks during the day. At the end of the day, the challenger was surprised and annoyed to find that the other fellow had chopped substantially more wood than he had. "I don't get it," he said. "Every time I checked, you were taking a rest, yet you chopped more wood than

I did." "But you didn't notice," said the winning woodsman, "that I was sharpening my ax when I sat down to rest."

– Lewis Sperry Chafer in "Grace"[34]

The issue:

I remember in my first few years of ministry, I was driven to do more and more in order to "get ahead." For me, more hours led to better work. The pastoral culture at the time honored such an approach. Those who "burned the midnight oil" were rewarded, while those who chose to use Fridays as their day off (in place of the normal Sabbath Day of Sunday) were often frowned upon. Those working on their days off were seen as hard workers and given a "job well done."

In recent years, the pendulum has switched a bit. Pastors are often encouraged to take time for themselves. The United Methodist Church has come to realize that escalated insurance premiums and family dysfunction are often a direct result of stressed out pastors who spend all of their time in the office and doing the "work" of ministry. A recent study from Duke University found that compared to their North Carolina neighbors, Methodist pastors had significantly higher rates of arthritis, diabetes, high blood pressure, and asthma. Obesity was 10 percent more prevalent among pastors.[35]

Members of our churches struggle with the same issues. From work to commitments after work, the days are far too short and packed with too many activities to accomplish in one day. It becomes a vicious cycle of busily getting the kids ready for school in the morning to working all day to attending kids activities after

34 Lewis Sperry Chafer. *Grace*. Kregel Publications, 2007.

35 Vitello, Paul. "Taking a Break From the Lord's Work." New York Times http://www.nytimes.com/2010/08/02/nyregion/02burnout.html?pagewanted=all&_r=0 (accessed May 5, 2017).

school to evening showers and homework. After 6 hours of sleep (the average amount for most Americans), the cycle begins again with the dawning of a new day. Our society teaches us subconsciously that longer hours and harder work are the keys to success. Those of us who make a decent take-home pay often work so hard that no time remains to enjoy our money. Others of us work hard just to make ends meet. The demands of feeding the family, buying needed necessities, and paying for the light bill leave us with little to nothing left in our bank accounts. By the time we could enjoy time for ourselves, we are far too tired to think about enjoying life.

In your occupation, do those in management encourage excessive work? Maybe it is not someone else. Maybe you feel driven to work hard and have little time left for other life priorities. If so, how does this affect your family life and friendships? How does this affect your ability to take time to enjoy days off, take family vacations, and recharge your batteries?

_____

_____

_____

Why is sabbath important?

Sabbath literally means, "rest." It is the understanding in Hebrew of the seventh day of the week. God created the world in six days. On the seventh, he stopped what he was doing to enjoy all that He created. The ultimate fulfillment for God was taking time to "smell the roses." Interestingly, when the phrase "stop and smell the roses" was first coined, it was changed from its original phrase. Golfer Walter Hagen was the first to use a similar phrase when he said, "You're here for a short visit. Don't hurry. Don't worry. And be sure to smell the flowers along the way" in the 1956 book *The Walter Hagen Story.*[36] Many believe that Hagen is responsible for helping to change the face of golf into the sport as we know it today. Even in the midst of his fame, fortune, and hard work, he realized the importance of enjoying that which was given to him. It's true! Earth was created for our enjoyment by God. God gave Adam and Eve everything under their dominion so they could not only live, but they could have a life of fun and fulfillment.

Beyond the enjoyment element, it's God's requirement for us. The Ten Commandments are very clear. In Exodus 20:8-11 (NIV) God tells Moses to write on the tablet, "Remember the Sabbath day by keeping it holy. Six days you shall labor and do all your work, but the seventh day is a sabbath to the Lord your God. On it you shall not do any work, neither you, nor your son or daughter, nor your male or female servant, nor your animals, nor any foreigner residing in your towns. For in six days the Lord made the heavens and the earth, the sea, and all that is in them, but he rested on the seventh day. Therefore the Lord blessed the Sabbath day and made it holy."

If Sabbath is for our enjoyment and God commands it, why do we not take time for Sabbath rest? Why do we insist on doing something that we are not naturally created to do? I am a big fan of baseball. Pitchers who pitch too many consecutive days risk injury. In the same respect, doctors are required to take a break after a certain time. A doctor who does not rest when he is tired becomes a danger to those who he is trying to help. In fact, when doctors are in the operating room, it is customary for them to take a

---

36 Hogen, Walter. *The Walter Hagen Story*, ch. 32, 1956.

pause or Surgical Time Out (STO). It means that they stop what they are doing before the surgery ever begins to catch their breath and refocus before they move forward. They confirm key details such as medications and which area is to be operated on. Studies have shown the pause or STO in the operating room is thought to lead to higher success rates in surgeries and avoiding complications.[37]

Scripture clearly teaches us again and again to keep the Sabbath. That's why it is found in the Ten Commandments. The further we are from our life pause or Sabbath, the more susceptible we are to straying from God's perfect and pleasing will for our lives.

Exodus 20: 8-11 (NIV) says:

"Remember the Sabbath day by keeping it holy. Six days you shall labor and do all your work, but the seventh day is a sabbath to the Lord your God. On it you shall not do any work, neither you, nor your son or daughter, nor your male or female servant, nor your animals, nor any foreigner residing in your towns. For in six days the Lord made the heavens and the earth, the sea, and all that is in them, but he rested on the seventh day. Therefore the Lord blessed the Sabbath day and made it holy.

Hebrews 4:9-11 (NIV) in the New Testament reaffirms this Old Testament law to keep the Sabbath. It continues in the spirit of Sabbath being a time of rest. "There remains, then, a Sabbath-rest for the people of God; for anyone who enters God's rest also rests from their works, just as God did from his. Let us, therefore, make every effort to enter that rest, so that no one will perish by

---

37 Lee, Steven, MD. "The Extended Surgical Time-Out: Does It Improve Quality and Prevent Wrong-Site Surgery?" The Permanente Journal. Spring 2010. https://www.ncbi.nlm.nih.gov/pmc/articles/PMC2912716/ (accessed April 19, 2017).

following their example of disobedience." True and lasting restoration cannot happen outside of Christian Sabbath rest.

What lessons can we learn from Scripture about God's desire for us to take Sabbath?

_____

_____

_____

How can we begin to change unhealthy life habits to allow more time for ourselves?

_____

_____

_____

What physical, emotional, and spiritual benefits might we realize if we take Sabbath?

_____

_____

_____

Value Your Vacation

Put it on the calendar early in the year. Catholic canon law requires priests — "unless there is a grave reason to the contrary" — to take a spiritual retreat each year, and four weeks of vacation.[38] In the United Methodist Church, pastors are required to take one week day off each week and a varying amount of annual vacation based on years of service. One to six years of service allows for two weeks and two Sundays off each year. Ministers with seven to fourteen years of experience are allowed to take three weeks and three Sundays. Fifteen plus years brings four weeks plus four Sundays. The church understands the necessity of time away as a precursor to effective ministry.

Vacations are a way to keep your tanks full. Nelson Searcy gives several practical tips on how to make the most of your vacations. Among his points is the need to rest, enjoy recreation, and re-calibrate.[39] The recreation aspect is supposed to be something that you enjoy doing that fills your tank. It's important for you to make memories that you can look back on, especially when we reach a difficult season in our everyday lives. Re-calibrating means that we refocus ourselves for the next season of worship, family life, and work that lay ahead. I think of it like a printer cartridge in an inkjet printer. It drives me crazy every time I buy a new printer because it makes me "re-calibrate." But, if I do not re-calibrate the printer, it will not print properly once I need it. It will print, but the ink will be smudged and unreadable. In the same way, we re-calibrate our thought lives so that we are prepared

---

38 Paul Vitello. "Taking a Brake From the Lord's Work." The New York Times. http://www..nytimes.com/2010/08/02/nyregion/02burnout.html?pagewanted=all&_r=0 (May 25, 2014)

39 Searcy, Nelson. *The Power of Vacation: Abandon Average by Keeping Your Tank Full.* Church Leader Insights. www.renegadepastors.com. April 2017, The Renegade Pastors Newsletter, p.12.

to face another season of work, family life, and work as we seek to be as effective as possible once we enter back into "normalcy."

Recommendations for Vacation:

I recommend that no minister take four weeks in a row, unless it is prearranged with their church's personnel committee and the church is okay with it. Cases exist where a minister's credentials were called in because he took his annual vacation time all at once without properly working with his church's personnel committee. In fact, it's hard for me to take two weeks in a row. My wife and I like to take one week after Christmas. Then we may take a week in the summer with the entire family. In doing this, we value our marriage and our kids. Sometimes when we go on our vacation after Christmas around New Year's, it is a chance for us to talk as adults and rest without our kids around. We usually take our third week of vacation in short increments (i.e.- the four-day family road trip!) once during the spring and once during the fall.

When vacation is already on the calendar early in the year, it allows you to look forward to it. Without predefined vacation dates, it is much easier to let your vacation slide or not take it at all. We may believe that our churches cannot run without us, but the truth is even more sinister: Sometimes they can't run with us! Our church is only as good as we are. Take the time!

Where do you want to go on vacation? List several places you would enjoy going and talk with your spouse about it.

_____

_____

Where can you take your spouse and children that they would enjoy? Talk with your spouse and children about their favorite places to visit. You may be surprised at some of the places they may mention. Allow their priorities to become your priorities sometimes! Write down their vacation destinations. Plan a vacation on a budget that you can afford. Don't talk about money the entire time, but do not overextend yourself either. Vacations are meant to refresh you and your family.

_____

_____

_____

Accountability for the sabbath

Allow your spouse and children to hold you accountable. I realize that if you are single, this approach may not work with spouse and children, but it can still work with friends who play golf with you or some sort of other expected activity on your day off. I remember being in the midst of a renovation project at Lyons. Our church acquired two pieces of property. One was a 1930 gas station near the Sanctuary's front corner. The gas station was in need of extensive repair, but our budget was very limited. I chose to do a great deal of the work myself, because it provided me an outlet to exercise as I swung a hammer and gutted the building. While I'm not as skilled at construction, demo is my game. About three quarters of the way through the demolition aspect, I wanted to finish quickly. I started putting in extra hours just so that I could get to the end more quickly. I decided one week to work on Friday. I was not going to allow working on Fridays to become a habit, but I wanted to get it done.

I arrived at the gas station at 7 a.m. (my usual time). I worked for three hours (I usually worked for four on most mornings before changing into my church clothes to do "regular" church work). At 10 a.m. that Friday, my wife showed up to the gas station with our two children, Maddux and Paxton, sitting in the back seat. The boys yelled out, "HEY DADDY!" I felt very convicted. While I value my ministry and want to do a fantastic job, it should not be at the expense of my family. I put the hammer down, went home and took a shower, and spent the rest of the day with the boys and my wife. Every time that I am tempted to work on my day off, I remember how much I love my boys and wife. It helps me to keep the proper perspective.

Do you allow work to encroach on your Sabbath? If so, how can you develop a plan to protect your Sabbath?

_____

_____

_____

Have good personal life systems.

In his book, *The Tribal Church*,[40] Steve Stroope provides 10 personal life systems to which every pastor should aspire. They are wonderful! Steve's systems have become my own personal life

---

40 Stroope, Steve. *Tribal Church*, B&H Publishing Group. 2012.

systems that I work through bi-weekly with my Life Coach. I added an eleventh that is Sabbath rest.

My systems ensure that I am staying on track and that I adapt to the proper perspective. Number one on the list is my daily Scripture reading and prayer time. Number eight on the list is my ministry. WOW! Seven priorities come before my ministry. It doesn't mean that ministry is not important (indeed it is, because I'll spend more time doing it each week than anything else!), but it does mean that priorities need to be in the proper order. God, my wife, my children, friendships, and mentoring are more important than my job. Without those seven items, the ministry can take over all of my time in a hurry. With priorities in the proper perspective, the ministry flows with much greater ease. Make sure that someone is holding you accountable for your life systems. When I speak to my Life Coach over the phone every other week, we discuss how I did in my personal life systems and areas for improvement over the coming two weeks.

What life systems or priorities do you value? Write down your priorities and begin to hold yourself accountable for keeping your priorities in the correct order.

_____

_____

_____

Learn how to delegate.

Live by the 80% rule. That is, if someone else can do it 80% as well as you can, hand it off. The problem is that we all want perfection. While we need to do our work well, we also need to empower someone else to know as much as we know in a given area (in time they may be able to do it better than we can!). Delegation is the key to Sabbath rest. When we have others working on our behalf, it allows us to take time for ourselves and our families.

Pastors may have "A" list and "B" list people working for them (both staff and volunteers), but only one pastor. Laity, you are only one person as well. Do not allow yourself to be burned out. It should always be the goal of the pastor and laity to teach someone else how to the job even better than he can!

There is only one of you. What do you need to teach someone else to do so that you do not over extend yourself? If you are overextended, what do you need to hand off so that you can return to a 40 hour work week?

_____

_____

_____

Summary:

Sabbath is crucial, not only for strong bodies but also for healthy relationships. It honors God because God commands us to take Sabbath.

Take Action:

Now Is the time to take Sabbath. JUST DO IT!

For More:

1) Check Out Nelson Searcy's resources entitled "The Thursday Midnight Rule" and "The Power of the Sabbath" (available at www.churchleaderinsights.com).

2) Pick up a copy of Walter Brueggemann's book *Sabbath As Resistance: Saying No to the Culture of Now.*

RECEIVE PRAYER REQUESTS BEFORE JOINING IN UNISON IN THE CLOSING PRAYER:

Dear Lord, thank you for loving me. Thank you for creating Sabbath for me. Show me how to rest as a way to strengthen myself for the days ahead. Help me to plan my vacation well in advance so that I can look forward to it and I can value my family. May I live a lifestyle of Sabbath rest as I am careful not to allow the things of this world to stress me out or to monopolize my time. I have 24 hours a day, like everyone else. I want to use my time wisely in a way that will bring glory to you. In Jesus' name, AMEN.

HOMEWORK: READ SESSION ELEVEN AND WRITE DOWN YOUR ANSWERS TO THE QUESTIONS FOR GROUP DISCUSSION BEFORE THE NEXT GROUP SESSION

www.RebuildBook.com

SESSION ELEVEN
Making It Personal within our Families: Marriage and Children

OPEN THE BIBLE STUDY SESSION WITH PRAYER. ASK GOD TO BLESS YOUR TIME TOGETHER.

ANSWER THE QUESTIONS FOR GROUP DISCUSSION BELOW:

Scriptures:

"For as a young man marries a young woman, so shall your sons marry you, and as the bridegroom rejoices over the bride, so shall your God rejoice over you."

- Isaiah 62:5 (NIV)

"The father of a righteous child has great joy; a man who fathers a wise son rejoices in him."

- Proverbs 23:24 (NIV)

Quote:

"God created marriage. No government subcommittee envisioned it. No social organization developed it. Marriage was conceived and born in the mind of God."

- Max Lucado[41]

---

41 "What Christians Want to Know." http://www.whatchristianswanttoknow.com/21-powerful-christian-marriage-quotes/ (May 5, 2017)

The Issue:

How Can My Spouse and I Enjoy a Godly Christian Marriage?

As I write this section, I write it more out of my own struggles than I do a sense of accomplishment. Billy Graham once wrote a best seller entitled *Storm Warning*. The general idea of the book is that in the midst of an ever-changing world, we need Jesus to calm the storms of our lives. I first read the book when I was a youth. At the time, The Billy Graham Evangelistic Association would allow you to become a member and then order the books that Billy had selected to send out to the subscribers who requested them. I sent in $5 per month. It probably did not cover the cost of the book, but it did make a lifelong impact upon a young reader.

Like the storm chasers in the Midwestern United States whose goal is to find a tornado and video it, we often chase storms in our lives. It's not purposeful, nor do we want to find our storms in our marriages and with our children; sometimes storms find us. They find us in arguments that erode the foundation of our marriage. They find us in the half truths that we speak. They find us when we feel we must be away from our family (when the truth is we can rework our schedules to allow for more family time).

Family is vitally important. As a husband and father, my decision to marry and have children comes with the decision to make family a priority. Do you remember what the Apostle Paul said in 1 Corinthians 7:8-14 (NRSV)?

"To the unmarried and the widows I say that it is well for them to remain unmarried as I am. But if they are not practicing self-control, they should marry. For it is better to marry than to be aflame with passion. To the married I give

163

this command—not I but the Lord—that the wife should not separate from her husband (but if she does separate, let her remain unmarried or else be reconciled to her husband), and that the husband should not divorce his wife. To the rest I say—I and not the Lord—that if any believer has a wife who is an unbeliever, and she consents to live with him, he should not divorce her. And if any woman has a husband who is an unbeliever, and he consents to live with her, she should not divorce him. For the unbelieving husband is made holy through his wife, and the unbelieving wife is made holy through her husband. Otherwise, your children would be unclean, but as it is, they are holy."

Paul understood the value of families. He knew that situations would arise not only between believing spouses, but also between believers and nonbelievers. As much as he wanted people to marry those who were equally yoked in the Lord, he knew that it was more important for the believing spouse to become a conduit of light and hope for the unbelieving spouse and their children. The other situation that might arise is that one spouse became a believer who lived in a home with an unbelieving spouse and children. The believing spouse then had the responsibility to share Christ his or her spouse and children.

How do you share your faith within the family? If you are in a relationship where your spouse is not a believer, how can you pray for them that they will come to a deeper relationship in Christ? If you are deeper in the faith than your spouse, how can you model a Godly Christian lifestyle so that your spouse and children can learn from your example?

No more vital issue exists in the world today than uplifting the family unit in the context of our Christian faith. With divorce rates now hovering above 50%[42] (that's one out of every two today) and co-habitations (persons living together outside of marriage) hovering around 25%[43] (that's one out of every four couples today), it is no wonder we live in a world experiencing further marital erosion. If someone is divorced or if someone cohabitates, Jesus loves you just as much. But, the ideal environment is to keep our Christian marriages thriving, to encourage Christian cohabiting couples to marry, and to make a happy Christian environment in which our kids can live and learn about Jesus.

What are some of the pitfalls of devaluing marriage? How can we reaffirm the ideal of Godly Christian marriage as we seek to uphold God's will for marriage?

---

42 American Psychological Association. http://www.apa.org/topics/divorce/ (May 25, 2014).

43 Aleccia, Jonel. "The New Normal: Cohabitation on the Rise, Study Finds." NBC News. http://www.nbcnews.com/health/health-news/new-normal-cohabitation-rise-study-finds-f1C9208429 (May 25, 2014).

I am a big fan of The Walk to Emmaus. It's a Christian weekend retreat. During a recent retreat that I worked, a female speaker stood up at the podium and talked about her experience in marriage. She said, "My husband and I made a commitment early in our marriage that we would never divorce." While I do give a shout-out to those who are in abusive relationships and understand that in very limited circumstances divorce is necessary, I applaud this lady. She was in her mid-30's at the time. She said that no matter how high or low that she and her husband may have been in their marriage, they understand that reconciliation was their only option. If divorce were an option, at times she would be ready to run for the door, because she and he sometimes disliked each other that much.

How do you respond to the phrase that "love is a commitment and not an emotion?" Sometimes we do not feel "in love." How do we stay committed to our marriage as we seek to fall back in love with our spouse?

_____

_____

_____

Marriage is important. Every seven years, we experience a natural "marriage cycle." This means that every seven years, we are tempted either to grow closer to one another or to grow apart . . . the choice is ours. If you look at how long people are married and when they divorced, most breakups happened on a seven-year cycle (year 7, year 14, year 21, etc.). After seven years, the children are often born and of a very young age. This is the first bump in the road. After 14 years, the kids are of adolescence age and financial demands find a peak. The is the second bump. If couples manage to make it through year 21 (when kids go off to school and the couple has the "empty nest syndrome"), the couple is much more likely to make it for the long haul. Perhaps by then a couple says to each other (even if not verbally!), "Well, I've made it this long with you, I might as well stick it out for the long haul!"

Do you find the seven-year cycle to be accurate? Have you noticed it in your life or the lives of someone that you know and love? How do we stay strong when marital drift occurs?

_____

_____

_____

There are several keys to maintaining a happy marriage.

1)

First, while mentioned in another part of the book, the divorce rate for couples who pray together is less than 1%. That's remarkable! If you want a solid marriage, pray! Nothing works better than inviting God to be the glue that holds us together.

2)

Second, make date nights MANDATORY! It's not optional. What you do on date night is up to you, but here are several suggestions. Do not take the kids. Make it at least two hours. Talk to each other for at least one hour of the date. In the beginning you may not know what to say, but it will come! And, while it may be tempting to make it sexual (or not!), I encourage you to practice nonsexual touch like holding hands and touching during the movie. These sorts of touch are often neglected, but they are vitally important when it comes to nonverbal communication. Women especially need to feel the communication that says, "I love you for more than just sex." If they do not feel loved beyond the physical connection, often it will lead to conflict elsewhere within the marriage.

3)

Third, couples need to have fun together. Erin and I started a few years ago to take a vacation with just the two of us right after Christmas each year. Often it is a chance to reconnect on a much deeper level. With three children, the obligations of taking care of them often leave a gap between the communication that we want and where we currently find ourselves. While it sometimes takes a little while on the vacation for us to reconnect, by the end we go back into our marriage ready for the next challenge. One year we took a road trip to the Orange Bowl where my beloved Florida State Seminoles played football. Then we drove down to Key West to soak in some rays on the beach while the rest of our friends at home enjoyed the briskness of the winter season.

4)

Fourth, couples should work on their finances together. As a rule, ten percent goes to the church (the tithe) and ten percent should go directly to savings for retirement. Debt should be retired as quickly as possible and money should be set aside for emergencies. Dave Ramsey will tell you that you should put aside 3 months of your monthly salary for emergencies. This will allow you to make it through should you experience periods of unemployment or other unexpected expenses. Finances are one of the most contentious issues in the marriage. Coming to a Christian understanding of managing money is not only wise, it may save your marriage. Check out the resources offered by Dave Ramsey and those offered by a host of other groups including Crown Financial.

5)

Fifth, couples should work on how they will raise their children. I remember the first time that I spanked Maddux. He is our oldest child. Spanking was an accepted practice in the Giddens' household during my childhood years. Erin does not like spanking. She believes that while it is okay to pop on the hand and to discipline through such methods as time out, spanking causes unwanted side effects in our children. She believes that our children may not feel loved or appreciated as much. In reading about spanking, I remember one author saying that spanking may cause the child to carry with them unnecessary baggage later in life.

Through research and discussion, Erin and I now agree on proper (and improper) methods of disciplining our children. While Erin and I still have a few rough patches from time to time, our communication on this issue has kept us from numerous arguments and conflicts. Beyond discipline, parents need to discuss how they will share their faith with their kids. They need to talk about what they want their kids to know about money management. Heaven forbid, children also need to hear their parents talk about God's intended roles for them in sex and dating. For too long, Christian parents relinquished that job to television and secular society. It is time that we take the reigns back when it comes to teaching our kids about God's intended purpose for dating and sex.

6)

Sixth, don't be afraid to ask for help BEFORE the crisis. The unfortunate truth is that most of us wait until there is a huge problem before we seek help. With our cars, we change the oil every 3,000 or so miles as a preventative measure. With the color copier in your office, office supply stores regularly advertise that if we do more than X amount of copies a day, the machine will tear up. As a preventative measure, we buy a large enough copier to handle the volume of copies we need to make. Knowing that there are limits to our skills and abilities in marriage, why not take preventative measures to save our marriages? We all value our privacy and want to put on a good appearance for the outside world. We want everybody to think everything is okay when it's not. And, the sadder truth is that everyone knows when we get a divorce. Divorces are very public. Take preventative steps to keep your marriage happy before you lose your marriage all together!

Which of these practical action steps can you implement or reaffirm in your marriage right now? Make a list of action steps.

_____

_____

_____

How Can I Raise Godly Children?

1)

First, teach your children about God. In his book *It Starts in the Family,*[44] Steve Stroope tells us that church should not be where faith starts . . . it starts in our families. Steve's book is a

---

44 Stroope, Steve. *It Starts At Home*, B&H Publishing Group. 2010.

compelling look at ways in which we invest in the lives of our children at home. Someone once said that the children are not the future of our church, THEY ARE THE CHURCH now! I believe it! We no longer live in a world where children and adults know the stories of Moses and Jonah. Many people do not know the true Christmas Story beyond what they see in the commercialized world. Parents have the extraordinary task of raising children in the Christian faith. Erin and I love bedtime Bible stories books. They simplify the stories and some even put the Biblical stories, into poetry. Sometimes, Maddux and Paxton finish the sentence as we recite the poem!

2)
    Second, we should teach our children financial management. While I'm already at church most Sunday mornings, Erin gives the boys a quarter and asks them to put it in their church Sunday School offering plate. In time, we will give them chores to do that will teach them further money management. They may earn a few dollars, yes, but they also will need to put ten percent of their allowance into the offering plate while saving ten percent for another purpose. While the ten percent savings can be used as they would like, Erin and I will encourage them to find a project that they want to give to and donate (like a water well in Africa or another mission). The goal is for our children to know that they can live off of 80% of their income. It's God's money entrusted to us.

3)
    Third, spend time with your children. Presence is one of the greatest gifts that we can give to our children. Hug them. Hold them close. Be at their sporting events, plays, and activities. Talk to them about what's going on in their world and listen with an

open mind. Don't criticize too quickly. It may be easy to criticize! If your children honestly answer your questions, give them a chance to be original. Value supper time and make a conscious choice to sit at the table with your entire family. I like the television show "Blue Bloods." At the end of each show, Tom Selleck and his television family (who are Catholic Christians) sit around the table and enjoy a meal and conversation. This is one area in which Hollywood got it right!

4)

Fourth, children should be able to escape current family dysfunction. I believe that too often we pass our "dirty laundry" down to our children. Erin and I are working hard to make sure that some of the less than helpful habits that we inherited do not go on to our children. We want our children to know that they can achieve anything that they put their minds to with God's help. We also want them to know that we are their biggest supporters. Family dysfunction can come in many forms and can be very subtle. If you are not sure of your blind spots, seek out a trained professional who can help you to identify these areas and then help you deal with them before you pass them along to your children.

What practical steps can you implement with your children (either listed here or maybe even others!)? Make a list.

_____

_____

_____

Summary:

Sharing a strong Christian marriage and raising our children in the context of a Christian home is vitally important. We can employ practical methods to value our marriages and our children.

Take Action:

Make the steps mentioned above commonplace in your home. It will cement the marriage and family that God desires for you to enjoy!

For More:

1) Check out Greg and Erin Smalley via www.smalleymarriage.com
2) Read Steve Stroope's *It Starts at Home*
3) Visit www.drivefaithhome.com (Steve Stroope's family resource website)
4) Read ALL of Dave Ramsey's resources including *Smart Money, Smart Kids* and *The Total Money Makeover.*
5) Encourage your church to participate in either Crown Financial (crown.org) or Dave Ramsey's Financial Peace University.

RECEIVE PRAYER REQUESTS BEFORE JOINING IN UNISON IN THE CLOSING PRAYER:

Dear Lord, thank you for our families. Even though they are not perfect, they are created by you. Strengthen our marriage as I make a commitment to growing in my

relationship with you daily and sharing your love with my spouse and children. Help me to realize that marriage is a commitment and that being in love takes continual effort. Show me how to raise my children in a Godly Christian environment so that they may love you as well. In Jesus' name, AMEN.

HOMEWORK: READ SESSION TWELVE AND WRITE DOWN YOUR ANSWERS TO THE QUESTIONS FOR GROUP DISCUSSION BEFORE THE NEXT GROUP SESSION

www.RebuildBook.com

SESSION TWELVE
Personal Evangelism:
Sharing Our Faith
with Non Believers and Uncommitted Believers

●————————————————————————●

OPEN THE BIBLE STUDY SESSION WITH PRAYER. ASK
GOD TO BLESS YOUR TIME TOGETHER.

ANSWER THE QUESTIONS FOR GROUP DISCUSSION
BELOW

Scripture:

"The King will reply, 'Truly I tell you, whatever you did for one of
the least of these brothers and sisters of mine, you did for me'."

- Matthew 25:40 (NIV)

Quote:

"You have nothing to do but to save souls. Therefore spend and be
spent in this work. And go not only to those that need you, but to
those that need you most. It is not your business to preach so
many times, and to take care of this or that society; but to save as
many souls as you can; to bring as many sinners as you possibly
can to repentance."

- John Wesley[45]

---

45 John Wesley Quotes. https://m.facebook.com/notes/john-wesley/john-wesley-
quotes/163177167059591/ (May 5, 2017).

The Issue:

We now live in a world where Christians sharing their faith is not the rule. Christians sharing their faith is the exception to the rule. A recent LifeWay study found that while 80 percent of those who attend church one or more times a month believe they have a personal responsibility to share their faith, 61 percent have not told another person about how to become a Christian in the previous six months.[46] Christians as a whole want to share their faith, but they do not do it. I believe that often it's because churches do not give opportunities for people to accept Christ, we do not teach how to share a testimony, and we do not give people the tools to help someone else to accept Christ for himself.

When was the last time you shared your faith with someone? Have you ever "saved" someone else by sharing the sinner's prayer, the Roman's Road, or a similar way for someone to come to faith in Jesus Christ?

_____

_____

_____

If you have shared your faith, how does it make you feel when you win a soul for Jesus and the Kingdom of God?

_____

---

[46] Lifeway Christian Research. http://www.lifeway.com/Article/research-survey-sharing-christ-2012 (accessed May 6, 2017).

_____

_____

Combine the above statistics with the understanding of "church hopping," and we can see why such an epidemic of church decline exists in America. As a world Church, we are not making disciples as needed. Church growth often happens not because of first-time decisions to Christ, but rather because we borrow from someone else's flock. While I do not mind the transfer of members from one church to another if they see that they can be better fed elsewhere or a family moves to a new town, too many members of existing congregations move to a new congregation out of convenience. Like a marriage, ups and downs in church membership occur that require our commitment to solve. And like marriage, we may not agree with every decision that is made, but we should be committed nonetheless.

How do you grow your church? Are the majority of new members within your church transfers from other churches or are they new believers who come to faith in Jesus Christ?

_____

_____

_____

How can you make an effort to be more proactive in bringing in new believers as the most substantial pipeline to growing your church?

_____

_____

_____

The other major source of difficulty in the church of America is found in a group that I will term "uncommitted." Uncommitted Christians are those who admit they are Christians, but they do not have a church home. It is estimated that only 20% of current Christians in America regularly attend church.[47] They may say they know Christ, but the fruit of their relationship with Him is far from evident. They are a group primed for discipleship and a closer walk with Jesus. They are waiting for someone to reach out and invite them to church.

When was the last time you invited someone to come to church? How can you be more proactive in actively recruiting a non-attender to come to your church? How do you invite someone to church who claims to be a Christian already but who is not associated with a church?

_____

_____

_____

---

47 Samuel, Stephanie. "Churches Dilemma: 80 percent of Flock Inactive." The Christian Post. http://www.christianpost.com/news/authors-pastors-must-go-after-lost-sheep-to-increase-church-participation-51581/ (May 6, 2017)

Why Is Personal Evangelism Important?

Jesus commands it. Look no further than Jesus himself. Matthew 28:19 says, "Go and make disciples." (NIV) We often allow our need to be comfortable to outweigh our need to share Jesus. Jesus did not give us an option. He said, "Go do it!" I've always loved this passage of Scripture because right after Jesus tells them to "Go and make disciples," we find that "some doubted." WOW! "Some doubted"! I take it to mean that while the disciples knew what they had to do and they were equipped with the tools to do it, it was still hard! They did not want to put in the sweat equity that would lead to Christian conversions. In Acts, the church took off on the day of Pentecost when the Holy Spirit descended upon the believers and each spoke in their own native language. Conversions happened not because of the people's ability, but because of the power of the Holy Spirit working through the people.

Sharing Jesus with others is essential, but only as we do it by the power of the Holy Spirit. When we feel uneasiness in telling someone about Jesus, that's when the Holy Spirit comes in and gives us the ability to reach beyond our comfort zones and share the love of Jesus anyway. In my 11 life systems that my Life Coach holds me accountable for, I am continually asked if I shared Jesus with someone else in the last two weeks. Sometimes I do share Jesus with two non-Christians, and sometimes I miss the mark.

Knowing that someone holds me accountable is a huge incentive for me to share Christ. I do not want to disappoint my Life Coach, and I do not want to disappoint myself. One day I was shopping at Big Lots and I shared Jesus with one of the guys working at the cash register. It was a great moment! After I shared with him what church I was buying the chairs for, it became an opening to invite him to church. I then said as a passing phrase, "God loves you and I'm so glad that I got to meet you today." Thinking I was about to walk off, he stopped me and said, "Tell me more." I did tell him much more, and we ended with a prayer. It was so simple, and the opened door was readily there. I needed to walk through it.

With seven billion people in the world today and only two billion Christians, a greater need than ever before calls us to share Jesus. Christianity as a whole in America is in decline. The population continues to increase exponentially, but the Christian population continues to decline.

What will we do to reverse this trend and to make sure that we're making Christians out of those who do not already know Jesus?

_____

_____

_____

What will be your Personal Evangelism goal every two weeks? Write it down:

_____

_____

_____

Who can hold you accountable for this goal? Write their name down and contact them. Ask them to pray for you and to ask you about whether or not you achieved your goal.

_____

_____

_____

Practical Steps to Sharing Jesus:

1)

Receive Jesus as your personal Lord and Savior. Do you want to know Jesus as Your Lord and Savior? Do you yearn to experience the Lord's comforting presence, power, and wisdom? That's good, because God loves you and wants to have a personal relationship with you forever.

The problem is . . . one thing separates you from a relationship with God—sin. You and I sin whenever we fail to live by the Lord's holy standard. In fact, Romans 3:23 (NIV): "All have sinned and fall short of the glory of God." Furthermore, Romans 6:23 explains that the penalty for sin is death—separation from God in hell forever. No matter how hard we try, we cannot save ourselves or get rid of our sins. We can't earn our way to heaven by being good, going to church, or being baptized (Eph. 2:8-9).

Understanding how helpless we are because of our sins, God sent His only Son, Jesus, to save us. Jesus Christ lived a perfect, sinless life, and then died on the cross to pay the penalty for our sins (Rom. 5:8). Three days later, He rose from the dead— showing that He had triumphed over sin and death once and for all.

So how can you know God? It all starts with accepting Jesus Christ as your Lord and Savior. Jesus Christ provides a relationship with the Father and eternal life through His death on the cross and resurrection (Rom. 5:10).

Romans 10:9 promises, "If you confess with your mouth Jesus as Lord, and believe in your heart that God raised Him from the dead, you will be saved." If you have not yet begun your personal relationship with God, understand that the One who created you loves you no matter who you are or what you've done. He wants you to experience the profound depth of His care.

Therefore, tell God that you are willing to trust Him for salvation. You can tell Him in your own words or use this simple prayer: "Lord Jesus, I ask You to forgive my sins and save me from eternal separation from God. By faith, I accept Your work and death on the cross as sufficient payment for my sins. Thank You for providing the way for me to know You and to have a relationship with my heavenly Father. Through faith in You, I have eternal life. Thank You also for hearing my prayers and loving me unconditionally. Please give me the strength, wisdom, and determination to walk in the center of Your will. In Jesus' name, Amen."

2)

Second, churches should offer opportunities to accept Christ. If your preacher does not offer a chance for you to know Jesus (either through an altar call, new member class, or other method), hold your pastor accountable. Pastors more than ever before need to lead their churches to Jesus. The church is not the building or the steeple. The church is the people. If the building ceases to exist and all that's left are the people, we might start to find the true church once again. The church's sole role in the world should be to know Christ and to make Him known.

3)

Third, learn how to share your testimony. If your church does not regularly offer opportunities for you to share your testimony, hold your pastor accountable. Sharing our testimony connects non-Christians and less-committed Christians with Jesus. Many people take the approach that "if they can do it, so can I!" Remember that many people do not know how badly that they need Jesus until you paint the picture for them, by sharing how much Jesus has done for you and how much Jesus loves you.

4)

Fourth, tell someone else about Jesus every two weeks. I would love for you to do as I do, sharing Jesus with two others every two weeks. But, make a reachable goal and go for it! Allow the Holy Spirit to accompany you when you go. I often share my faith when I least expect it.

When working on the gas station in Lyons, people would walk by and start a conversation with me. One day a guy said, "Hey man, what are y'all doing here?!" I responded, "We're making the building look like it looked back in 1930 when it was a gas station." The guy said, "That ain't never been a gas station! It was a car wash!" The man was actually correct that two years before the church bought it, it was in fact a car wash . . . but I did not argue the point! We continued our conversation with him thinking it was a car wash and me thinking it was a gas station. I was able to share Christ with him and pray with him. It was an awesome moment. How many of us have a need to be right over a need to share Christ? In all of our lives and more, the point of all that we do should be to share Christ . . . PERIOD. When we see life from the proper perspective, it allows us to have the right priority in JESUS.

What is your Personal Evangelism plan? Write it down.

_____

_____

_____

Summary:

Sharing Jesus is not a "plus" . . . it is a requirement for those who know Him.

Take Action:

1) If you have made the decision to follow Jesus as your personal Lord and Savior, congratulations! You have made the best decision you will ever make—one that will change your life forever! Please let us know by emailing us at decision@rebuildbook.com so we can rejoice with you and pray for you.[48]

2) Share Jesus with one person every two weeks and have someone hold you accountable for doing so.

3) Hold your church's pastor accountable for offering opportunities to know Jesus, learn how to share your testimony, and learn how to pray with someone else to receive Jesus.

---

[48]Stanley, Charles. "How Do I Accept Jesus As My Savior?" InTouch.org
https://www.intouch.org/read/content/how-do-i-accept-jesus-as-my-savior (accessed April 25, 2017)

For more:

Robert Coleman's *The Master Plan of Evangelism* was first written in 1963. The latest edition came out in 2010. It begins with a foreword by Billy Graham and quote from (of all people!) Karl Marx. Marx said, "Philosophers have only interpreted the world differently. The point is to change it." While Marx may not be the embodiment of the Christian faith, Coleman says that changing the world is exactly what we Christians should be about. He's right! Let's change our world for Jesus. It's still possible . . . one life changed at a time.

RECEIVE PRAYER REQUESTS AND JOIN TOGETHER IN UNISON IN THE CLOSING PRAYER

Dear Lord, we are grateful for the gift of Jesus Christ and how He died on the cross for our sins so long ago. Today, we commit our lives to you and living for Jesus everyday. We pledge to take up the mantle of sharing Jesus with all whom we meet. Show us those people with which you would want us to share our faith. Give us the confidence and boldness to win souls for Christ. May we do all we can to grow your Kingdom here on this earth. In Jesus' name, AMEN.

www.RebuildBook.com